The Essential Guide to Creating a Chinese-Style Garden

DESIGN A LANDSCAPE FOR THE SOUL IN YOUR OWN BACKYARD

FOR SHANGHAI PRESS & PUBLISHING DEVELOPMENT COMPANY
President and Publisher: Wang Youbu
Editorial Director: Wu Ying
Editors: Ye Jiasheng, Kirstin Mattson, Shen Xunli

Text and Illustrations: Gao Yonggang
Photographs: Gao Yonggang, Getty Images, Quanjing, shutterstock.com, istockphoto.com
Translation: He Jing, Huang Zhihua, David Specchio
Interior Designers: Yuan Yinchang, Li Jing, Hu Bin

ISBN 978-1-60652-161-8
Library of Congress Cataloging-in-Publication Data is available upon request.

FOR READER'S DIGEST
Executive Editor, Trade Publishing: Dolores York
Cover Designer: Jennifer Tokarski

THE READER'S DIGEST ASSOCIATION, INC.
President and Chief Executive Officer: Mary Berner
President of Asia Pacific: Andrea Martin
President and Publisher, U.S. Trade Publishing: Harold Clarke

Printed in China by Shenzhen Donnelly Printing Co. Ltd.

1 3 5 7 9 10 8 6 4 2

The Essential Guide to Creating a Chinese-Style Garden | DESIGN A LANDSCAPE FOR THE SOUL IN YOUR OWN BACKYARD

Gao Yonggang

The Reader's Digest Association, Inc.

Pleasantville, New York / Montreal / Sydney

Preface

A Chinese-style garden, drawing on centuries of tradition and refinement, can bring an elegant touch to a yard no matter where in the world it is located. This book will help you to understand the essence of the Chinese-style garden, whose inward-facing, refined esthetic can contrast greatly with its typically open, geometric Western counterpart. Inside, you will find everything you need to know about Chinese-style gardens, from their origin, rich tradition and artistic conception to the practical application of techniques and patterns.

Western-style homes often feature yards where family members can barbecue, come together and relax on weekends or holidays. Such yards are generally spacious and simple, with a focus on utility and socializing. Thanks to their frequent use of geometric forms, they tend to create a sense of order, consistency, balance and proportionality, and highlight the esthetic of the man-made.

In contrast to the openness and flamboyant style of their Western counterparts, Chinese courtyard homes are more inward and reserved, reflecting the focus of China's traditional elite, the literati. They offer an exclusive sanctuary where people can revive their bodies and indulge their souls. These spaces were originally created as a place for literati to perform the traditional "eight activities"—to live leisurely, to farm and read, to seek self-edification, to build character, to admire beautiful things, to visit, to daydream, and to express feelings and sentiments.

Enclosed by high walls, Chinese courtyards emphasize the reclusive nature of home, and the commitment to a greater harmony between man and nature. In traditional Chinese homes, doors are often situated separately in the front and back yard. High walls and black tiles close off the inner world, giving outsiders plentiful scope to imagine what is within. As an ancient poem says, "the garden cannot hold in the beauty of spring," and plants stretching beyond walls allow outsiders a tantalizing glimpse of what's inside. Thus, contrary to the more open Western-style home, Chinese courtyard homes attach emphasis to independence, privacy, and a sense of self-indulgence.

The difference between Chinese and Western cultures is evident in their respective means of presenting courtyards. For example, in the West, houses are encircled by yards, while the opposite is the case in China—the house encircles the yard. In addition, harmony between man and nature is stressed within the Chinese garden,

where winding paths lead to sheltered hollows. In contrast, Western yards often regulate nature, using an open, simple geometry. Chinese gardens focus more on creating an "artistic mood," while to their Western counterparts, utility and order can be of most importance.

Admittedly, they do have many things in common. Water, for example, is a recurrent theme in both. Western yards emphasize being close to water as a necessary part of everyday life and recreation. Water, essential to a private home, often appears in pragmatic forms, such as a swimming pool or a fountain. At noon, basking in bright sunlight, the sparkling, rippling water adds movement and life to the backyard. Water is used quite differently in Chinese courtyards. Split by bridge, corridor, pavilion, platform or embankment, it takes many versatile forms, such as a small pond or zigzagging stream. Houses are surrounded by water or sit adjacent to it, or are even built around it. The smart integration of water landscape and architecture brings about a natural charm, where even the simple act of sipping tea becomes an indulgence.

In today's world, where cultures of all nationalities are converging, and the influence of the East is expanding day by day, is it possible to fuse Chinese and Western styles together, while preserving their respective characteristics? The use of Chinese elements in a Western garden, even if it is just in a corner or a small section, creates a unique and inviting scene. What a pleasant surprise it would be to find Chinese features, such as dappled shadows, stone alleys and ice crackle windows, within a Western courtyard featuring sheds, awnings, platforms, flower stands or arcades. And how refreshing it would be to see Chinese landscaping elements —small bridges, flowing streams, artificial hills, flower ponds, waterside houses or pavilions—in a Western garden comprised of lawns, hedges, fountains and architectural accessories. Whether the integration of such diverse forms actually works depends on the garden designer's skills. But surely, the successful synthesis of the two produces a real home for the soul.

Contents

Introduction

The three-thousand-year history of Chinese gardens traces back to the earliest written records in the Shang (1600BC–1046BC) and Zhou (1046BC–256BC) dynasties. Over the many centuries, gardens have developed diversified and individualized styles, and often feature forms with distinct regional characteristics.

What Is a Chinese Garden?

The Chinese garden boasts a rich history and astonishing accomplishments. It has undergone an evolution in functionality (from simplicity to complexity) and scale (from small to big). Most importantly, gardens must be a relatively independent space, where thanks to the design and planning of innovative individuals, a series of esthetic features and construction approaches, including artificial hills and water landscapes, are used to construct surroundings for the appreciation of visitors. With regard to functionality, gardens focus on bringing pleasure.

In southern China, the concept of the garden is in fact derived from today's patio—a small area inside the house. The patio, enclosed by walls, ensures privacy while also enjoying plentiful natural wind and light. It is common to grow flowers and grass in its corners or around its borders, for the pleasure of family members. If space allows, an artificial hill or a pond can be built. What exotic fun it is to sit on the patio and sip a cup of tea.

In northern China, the evolution of the courtyard house marks a transition from "court" to "yard." The "yard" refers to the piece of land enclosed by walls, with the same function as the patio in the south. However, courtyards are far more spacious than patios, allowing one to grow flowers or even build platforms in them, offering more enjoyment compared to patios.

Chinese-style gardens vary in scale. Small ones are mostly a singular activity space with simple architecture and a unified theme. On the other hand, bigger gardens boast a diverse range of functions. They can offer a platform for visitors to hold meetings, dine outside, watch plays and appreciate the full moon. A small number of private gardens are far more spacious than the previous two types, and exist as their own entity, completely independent of a dwelling or ancestral halls. A large-scale royal garden features not only great views and landscapes, but also courts where emperors would handle politics, dwellings where royal families slept, and halls where ancestors were worshipped. It is therefore a garden complex featuring buildings of versatile patterns.

Types of Chinese-style Gardens

Throughout thousands of years of history, Chinese gardens have appeared in different guises—royal gardens, temple gardens, natural gardens and private gardens. These gardens vary according to diverse political, economic, cultural, geographic and climate conditions. Each type of garden boasts its own unique characteristics. For example, royal gardens are grand, splendid, and magnificent; natural gardens are an integral whole with beautiful mountains and clear waters; temple gardens, making full use of local conditions, are quiet and deep; private gardens are refined, simple and elegant. Gardens may also be divided into northern gardens, southern gardens and Lingnan gardens, based on their geography and the garden design tradition to which they belong.

1) Royal Garden

While the origin of royal gardens in China dates back several thousand years, today's top tourist destinations are mostly works of the Qing dynasty (1644–1911). Located around Beijing and Hebei Province, such royal gardens boast a quiet, secluded environment and breathtaking views. They often adopt two patterns. One is the court for dwelling and holding audience with the emperor, built in the front with convenient transport; the other is the pleasure park and rest area, built in the back. The Summer Resort, the Summer Palace and the Yuanmingyuan Garden are notable examples of the latter. The artistry of royal gardens reached an unprecedented height in terms of architectural construction and integration with nature, boasting unique qualities and characteristics.

All royal gardens are large. Take the Yuanmingyuan Garden and the Summer Palace as examples; the former occupies over 200 hectares, while the latter takes up around 300 hectares. Built upon natural mountains and lakes, a royal garden can provide views as beautiful as those produced by nature, with some enhancements. In keeping with the garden's splendid style, the buildings inside are always large in both size and number, to help accentuate the beauty of architectural forms. Thanks to the exploitation of symmetry, high towers, serene buildings, stained glass and heavy objects, royal buildings appear dignified, steady, resplendent and magnificent, qualities which are in full display in royal gardens.

As China is a vast country with varied, rich resources, its south and north are markedly different from each other, as will be discussed in the following section. Back in the mid-Ming dynasty, northern gardens began to borrow some elements of the southern garden's distinctive style. With the addition of these garden elements—such as corridors, water galleries, bridges, pavilions, white walls, carved windows and flower windows—the artistry of the royal garden reached an unrivaled peak.

Yuanmingyuan Garden (Old Summer Palace) is located in the east of Beijing's Haidian District. A legacy of the Ming dynasty, it was constructed in 1707, 46th of the reign of Emperor Kangxi of the Qing dynasty, and constantly expanded, improved by his succeedors, used as a place for emperors to relax and to meet with officials. It was further improved by Emperor Qianlong, who made six tours to regions south of the Yangtze River and brought back many valuable treasures, including rare stones and plants. During the sixty years of his reign he spent a lavish amount of money in decorating the palace and construction was ongoing. In 1860, British and French forces invaded Beijing, setting fire to the famous palace, and only the ruins remain. Yuanmingyuan Garden covered about 5,000 *mu* (one *mu* is approximately 667 square meters) with a perimeter of over 20 kilometers. There were over 140 important buildings, more than 100 key scenic spots, and a myriad of famous rock mountains, outlandish stones and rare plants. The palace was then rightly known as the "palace of palaces" by Westerners.

2) Temple Garden

Within the big family of Chinese gardens, temple gardens outnumber royal and private gardens several hundred times over. The category escapes constraints shared by royal and private gardens, as its members spread across scenic spots and historical sites, famous for their beautiful natural environment. In a temple garden, natural and man-made beauty come together perfectly, thanks to the sophisticated integration of natural scenery and man-made architecture, as well as the organic connection between the inside and the outside.

Temple gardens can be found in mountain valleys or on peaks, deep inside mountain areas, on cliffs, or within caves. They are designed in a secretive and non-exposed manner, always making full use of local conditions, which gives each a unique feeling of its own. For example, at a temple garden located on a mountain top, visitors can benefit from the advantage of height, to enjoy clear views, open horizons, and a sense of standing above everything. It provides a good opportunity to see a beautiful skyline and a rare landscape of magical charm.

Nature and temples merging together can create a special type of spiritual ambience. Some temples are built in the open air, perhaps built in open land with good natural conditions or on a mountain. The area surrounding the temple may be reserved for visitors to take in the dramatic views. Take Putuo Mountain as an example. Located to the east of Zhoushan Island in Zhejiang Province, it is one of the top four destinations for Buddhists in China. Despite its small size, it provides a wonderful locale, facing the sea and situated on high ground. Boasting an unobstructed panorama, and rich layers of landscape, temples there are ideal places to appreciate breathtaking views.

An ancient temple hidden deep in the mountain is an iconic scene in China. A temple built in deep in the mountain valley, where trees grow and waters flow, may smartly utilize surrounding topography to capture distant views from different angles and positions. At the Lingyin Temple, adjacent to the West Lake in Hangzhou, the temple building complex is hidden behind lush and dense mountain trees. As a result, the tranquil and serene atmosphere of nature is preserved, accentuating the heavy religious air emanating from the temple.

Thanks to their clever use of local conditions, temple gardens can create spectacular landscapes. When you stand in a temple adjacent to a deep valley, or an abyss, or even a river, how thrilling it is to look down. At the temple in Leshan, the giant Buddha carved

Temples and gardens can be found in conjunction with many famous Chinese scenic spots. Pictured here is the Guanyin Cave, at the Hezhang Peak of Yandang Mountain in Zhejiang Province. At the entrance of the cave, one can find Tianwang Hall with four statues located there. There are 377 steps leading up to the top of the cave, which is the largest at Yandang Mountain. There is a temple within Guanyin Cave, which is set against rippling mountain tops and peculiar natural scenery. It is dark and cool in the cave, a strong contrast with the outside. This imbues the cave with a mysterious and religious atmosphere. It is indeed an ingenious choice of location for the temple.

out of a cliff, the stone stairs leading to the feet of the Buddha, and the pavilion built next to the cliff, all make a strange but enchanting scene.

Caves are another terrain-related feature of temple gardens. Vision inside a cave is limited, and the dim and damp atmosphere contrasts sharply with the outside landscape. Building a temple inside a cave provides a shelter which is warm in winter, cool in summer, and immune to wind and rain. In addition, it provides an element of surprise and enjoyment. For example, Guanyin Cave on Yandang Mountain in Zhejiang Province looks like a natural gallery cave from afar. Upon closer inspection, you will find the palace hall hidden inside. All the buildings are contained within the cave, a truly original masterpiece.

On the Four Seasons Mountain within the Shanghai Botanical Garden there are flowers blooming at all times of the year, so you can enjoy the beauty and variety of each season. The undulating ground and winding streams bring vibrancy to the garden.

3) Natural Garden

Natural gardens, as the name suggests, are based on natural landscapes with a certain degree of manual development. The original landscape is, for the most part, kept intact. Such gardens are big, versatile and completely open. The most typical examples include the West Lake in Hangzhou, the Slender West Lake in Yangzhou, the Xuanwu Lake in Nanjing, the Cui Lake in Kunming, and the Sun Moon Lake in Taiwan. Natural gardens have a size and scale much larger than that of private and temple gardens. They are for people to visit and have fun.

The value of natural gardens lies in their proper development and preservation. Excessive development must not be permitted to replace nature. Otherwise, the garden is really not natural at all. The location is crucial. Natural gardens are generally located in mountain areas, near lakes or other bodies of water, in either suburbs or rural areas. Making full use of natural landscape features, they contain plants, flowers, architectural accessories, pavilions and platforms, applying rational modifications, renovations, and finishing details to the original.

4) Private Garden

Private gardens, also known as residential or city gardens, are often built in secluded areas of a city while being linked with neighborhoods. Compared with other types, private gardens do not have natural landscapes to draw upon. Instead, they rely on manpower for digging rivers and ponds, applying stones and planting trees. In terms of artistic effects, they hope to create scenes that follow the traditional precept, "though man-made, still looks natural." In a private garden, meticulous efforts are made in concealing all man-made clues. There is a focus on the presence of buildings, pavilions and platforms; the important role played by artificial hills; the supporting role of flowers and plants; and creating a layered landscape. As a result, every corner forms a picturesque scene of its own, shaping a sophisticated but special garden art out of a small space.

In terms of size, natural gardens are the biggest, being followed in turn by royal, temple, and private gardens. Despite having the smallest size, private gardens thrive on attention to detail and breaking down space constraints. A myriad of faces are presented

In 1342, a disciple of the eminent monk Weize bought a piece of land to build his home. Weize's teacher, Master Zhongfeng, had begun his preaching at Lion Rock in Tianmu Mountain. Therefore, the garden, pictured here, was named the Lion Forest Garden.

within this small area, emanating a sense of culture, and embodying the essence of Chinese garden artistry.

Regional Variation

Owing to its vast territory and diverse climatic conditions, China has strong regional differences, in natural landscapes and architectural styles. Based on regional qualities, there are three types of garden—northern gardens, southern gardens and Lingnan gardens. The first category is widespread in Xi'an in Shaanxi Province, Luoyang and Kaifeng in Henan Province, Chengde in Hebei Province, Beijing, and Ji'nan in Shandong Province, from the mid to the downstream area of the Yellow River. Large and grand royal gardens located in Beijing are its most typical examples. The second category clusters around Yangzhou, Nanjing, Wuxi and Suzhou in Jiangsu, Hangzhou in Zhejiang, and Shanghai from the mid to the downstream area of the Yangtze River. Suzhou gardens and the region's many private gardens are its most typical examples. The third category can be found in Zhu River basin locations such as Chaozhou, Guangzhou, Dongguan, Shunde and Panyu in Guangdong Province.

The Summer Palace, located in the northwest of Beijing, covers about 300 hectares. Two natural scenic spots, Wanshou Mountain and Kunming Lake, are integrated into the palace, bringing a refreshing and grand quality. There are over 3,000 halls, gardens and buildings of various shapes and sizes. The palace is a paragon in Chinese gardens because all the naturalness is retained despite its man-made elements.

1) Northern Garden

Owing to the dry weather and cold winter in northern parts of China, gardens there are always grand, weighty and durable. As buildings feature thick walls and heavy roofs, materials used should be strong, giving an imposing and bold touch to the exterior. Green trees are the most popular option, in particular, pine and cypress. Strong colors such as red, green, blue and yellow are commonly used to produce a magnificent picture. Lush pines set off by blue sky with white clouds, together with yellow tiles and red columns, make the garden appear splendid and glittering.

The distinct features of northern gardens are most evident in royal gardens. With a precise layout and grandiose scale, they elevate the esthetic quality of garden architecture to an unrivalled level. They are splendid, noble, and luxurious. But they can also be seen as a bit showy and heavy, lacking a sense of flexibility and transparency.

2) Southern Garden

The weather in southern China is wet and rainy especially in the spring. In fact, a popular expression in Chinese links "Jiangnan," the regions south of the Yangtze River, with "spring rain," referring to its distinctive beauty during the season. Southern parts of China have high temperatures all year round, four distinctive seasons, and evergreen trees. Garden buildings always feature white walls, black tiles, maroon columns, small bridges, flowing waters and yards parted by corridors. Small gardens can generate a great deal of enjoyment. Flowers and plants bloom throughout the year. Their diverse and bright colors soften the plainness of white walls, acting as a transition point.

The design of the garden makes full use of local conditions, and often follows the concepts of "less is more" and "seeing the big through the small." In general, southern gardens are beautiful, light and smart. Blooming plants, lovely Tai Lake stones, corridors, water galleries, pavilion bridges, flat bridges, stone boats, pavilions, white walls, carved windows and tunnel doors come together to form a poetic and picturesque southern garden with a natural, simple, refreshing and elegant touch.

The three distinct features of southern gardens are most evident in private gardens. Firstly, the design and layout is flexible and diversified, using existing landscape features to allow for natural enjoyment, and striving to hide any artificial trace. Secondly, buildings are stylish and exquisite, equipping the small area with multiple attractions by creating a diverse array of scenery within the limited space. Thirdly, colors are light and elegant. Private gardens, also known as literati's gardens, have a refined ambience and are acclaimed for being a "soundless poem and a cubic painting," meaning the landscape is poetry without words and a work of art in three-dimensions.

In 1509, during the reign of Emperor Zhengde of the Ming dynasty, Minister Wang Xianchen was relieved of his duty and went back to his home town to build the Humble Administrator's Garden. Water takes up one-third of the area of the garden. In the center is the main building, and the garden's buildings are all surrounded by water. Objects in the garden are organized in a compact manner and their combination looks very natural. The garden is representative of those in southern China.

In the southernmost areas of China, such as here in Hong Kong's Kowloon Park, gardens are typically dotted with tropical plants, tall trees, deep ponds and dense flowers. The arbor here is different from those in Suzhou gardens in that it looks elongated and somber.

3) Lingnan Garden

The Lingnan area includes Guangdong Province, Guangxi Province and some parts of Hunan Province and Jiangxi Province. Boasting sound weather conditions, its winters are warm, summers are cool, plants are luxuriant, mountains are green, and waters are clear—a typical subtropical and tropical region. Due to such regional and climate characteristics, Lingnan gardens are always relaxing, comfortable and open.

The distribution of buildings in a Lingnan garden is continuous and consistent. Location, instead of flamboyance, is paramount. Two buildings are typically linked by a structure called a "cold alley," a roof-less structure with high walls on both sides, next to which flowers and bamboo are grown. When the wind comes, rains fall, and sun rises, the "cold alley" provides a welcoming shelter. Such "cold alleys" and "draughts" are effective solutions for heat reduction in houses.

Using another method for dealing with high temperatures, Lingnan gardens may have bridges that serve as passages, and water flows under floors or past halls. Thus, the nearby water causes the room temperature to lower, while family members can play with water and appreciate the aquatic views. A typical design features a boat hall set up in the center, with its inner hall facing a bridge; water flows around, further reducing the temperature.

Wood buildings in a Lingnan garden are mostly exposed. In response to the rainy, wet and hot weather in the region, carved decorations are often employed to help with ventilation and dampness reduction, and attention is paid to the protection of the buildings' exterior. As a result, sculptures and hollow ridge decorations are used. Lingnan ridge decorations are bold and unconstrained, boasting detailed carving, luxuriant decoration and bright colors, in perfect harmony with brick sculptures, stone sculptures, embedded porcelain and pottery.

This arbor in Kowloon Park is very typical of tropical areas.

In terms of themes, the dragon is the predominant pattern, with its lively and romantic serpentine body. Another major image is the giant fish; derived from the crocodile, it is a strong, powerful and energetic image. A new ridge decoration in the shape of a dragon's head and fish tail—reflecting the area's fishing-oriented way of life and the worshipping of dragons and fish—is becoming the crown jewel in Lingnan garden architecture.

How Is a Chinese Garden Different from Its European and Japanese Counterparts?

1) The Artistic Style of the Chinese Garden

The history of creating gardens in China is a rich and long one, with a focus on enjoyment and an appreciation of nature. Therefore, natural mountains and water elements are typical features of a Chinese garden. The overall layout should make full use of local conditions, with buildings constructed in accordance with natural forms.

A guiding principle is that the visitor should not be able to take in all scenes in just one gaze, but that the scenes should slowly unfold. Courtyards should have rich layers to reflect the important independent esthetic value of each landscape. Different artistic approaches to presenting scenery, such as "view borrowing," "view splitting," "view framing," "view leaking" and perspective, which are described further in later sections, are used to accentuate subtlety, depth, harmony and reserve. Unlimited enjoyment and pleasure is nurtured despite limited space.

Buildings often account for a large proportion of the garden. Based on the landscaping needs, they work in tandem with artificial hills, ponds and plants, to make a harmonious and beautiful garden vista. Their types, sizes, presence and styles are determined by geographic conditions. In addition, they are distributed in a staggered manner to interact with other architectural elements such as pavilions, Chinese belvederes. They bend and curve in line with the landscape, avoiding being straight, hard and edgy. There is a strong emphasis on natural changes and a sense of tempo.

Plants are a flexible option for making a beautiful garden. They may be arranged casually according to need, and may either stand alone or be scattered around. A plant standing alone tends to show off its individual beauty, a major attraction in the garden. Such designs must use plants that are beautifully styled, brightly colorful, large in size and long lasting. If it is used to provide protection against the sun, the plant must have a large crown and dense leaves. Plants scattered around may serve to support the garden's major features. Such plants must be attractive both as a whole and individually. Selection of flowers and plants should focus on the principles of "quality over quantity" and "the simpler, the better." Featuring plants with bright colors, an attractive fragrance and style is the ideal choice.

Water is a must-have element in building a garden. A garden cannot exist without it. Water landscaping in Chinese gardens mainly uses water that is calm on the surface, while flowing beneath. A glassy water surface contains quiet, stable and clean beauty. Dynamic water

Naturalness is an essential element to
Chinese gardens. The creativeness of a
garden is poetic and picturesque. The
garden is not only a "poem without words"
but also a "three-dimensional painting."
Garden designers are traditionally also
good painters.

On the mountains of Lion Forest Garden, there are many peculiar peaks and strange stones of different sizes and shapes. Most of them look like lions and take on different expressions. Ni Yunlin and Zhu Dejian, two famous painters, were consulted in designing the garden. The Lion Forest Garden is representative of the garden of a member of the literati with deep ties to the arts.

landscapes may also adopted to create a contrast. Stones or plants are used to split the water surface so that part of the water is hidden. Water slowly flows from stone gaps to add a dynamic touch, and enrich layers of landscape. Water landscaping in Chinese gardens is always based on natural conditions, with an artistic flavor markedly different from that of Western gardens.

As a re-creation of natural scenes in miniature, Chinese gardens deem the construction of artificial hills as a priority. They emphasize creating the typical beauty of nature in a limited space. Using the intriguing concept of "perfect imbalance," they adopt multiple ways of expression, such as turning a single stone into a feature, making an independent cliff or artificial hill, or even creating miniature chains of hills.

Selecting stones and stacking them are each arts in themselves. Stones have individual personalities that are categorized as "thin, leaky, thorough, wrinkled" as well as "clear, stubborn, ugly and clumsy." These categories, which are further discussed in chapter two, are the standard for judging both stone selection and stacking artistry.

In a Chinese garden, the limited space is divided into several scenic zones. Each zone has its own features, while still remaining linked to the others.

This garden at a Shanghai mansion was created by the author. It resembles a natural European garden.

Zoning can be created through the use of walls, carved windows, ponds, kiosks and pavilions. Even corridors and flower-pattern windows can be used to add perspective and layers, and show off the relatively independent esthetic of each zone. Techniques such as "view blocking" and "view borrowing" are commonly used to create different vistas with every step, along paths full of twists and turns.

2) The Artistic Style of the European Garden

The art of the garden in Europe, as represented by French gardens, excludes or subdues nature to produce rigorous rationality. European-style gardens follow geometric structures and mathematic relations in a meticulous manner, to produce a pattern-based garden layout.

In European gardens, buildings are the dominant player. A prominent building or a castle is usually located on the central axis of the garden, built in perfect symmetry. Several wide park avenues stretch out from the main building, decorated with flower terraces,

ponds, fountains and sculptures on both sides. The overall layout appears in strict geometric patterns. Passages are straight. Squares are set up at crossings. Ponds form part of the patterning, and within the ponds stand fountains with human and animal sculptures. Plants are trimmed to appear round, columned, coned or diamond shaped. Flower terraces also adopt shapes of geometric forms. The abundant use of flowers moderates the edges of trimmed plant beds. From a distance, a large lawn can resemble a carpet.

Unlike their Chinese counterparts, which seek a subtle and hidden beauty, European gardens favor overall symmetry. The goal is to present all components for appreciation in one, overarching glance. There are no layers; you do not wind your way from one contained view to another. You may need to climb high to appreciate the overall beauty of the garden.

All necessary elements of a European garden, including ponds, flowerbeds and lawns, work together to ensure integrity and harmony in numbers, through grouping of geometric forms. Contrary to

Objects found in ponds in a European garden, like those seen here, are often used in the gardens of Shanghai mansions. The European flowerbed requires constant attention, and the flowers are changed every season. The picture shows the author's own design.

the Chinese garden's pursuit of uniformity in spirit but difference in appearance, European gardens strive to achieve similarity in appearance, applying the principle that beauty in an object lies in the holy ratio between its parts. The Chinese admire curvy beauty, believing that only curves can reflect the irregularity of nature, while Westerners love straight lines. They see beauty in straight lines and geometry, and in the ability to create these forms through the use of nature. It is clear that Westerners and Chinese have differing theories, approaches and esthetic values in relation to garden design.

3) The Artistic Style of the Japanese Garden

The artistry of Chinese gardens was introduced to Japan together with Buddhism in the sixth century. The Japanese were influenced by the Chinese in building an island in a pond, which became the focal point of the typical Japanese home, and laid the foundation for the development of tea ceremony and Zen gardens. The art of the garden was imported to Japan at a time when it was already mature in China. In Japan, it was further developed to incorporate local influences, in particular using water, stone and sand, to promote garden artistry to a perfect peak, and form a distinct Japanese style.

Japanese gardens are often deeply reflective of the spiritual quality of nature, so that a spiritual essence is given to static objects. In addition, their use of colors and choice of plants is refined and may feature a muted color palette. The small home garden often reflects nature in a much more abstract manner than you would find in a Chinese private garden. Japanese gardens have several types that are in contrast to one another: the traditional Zen garden featuring sand waves; the classic stroll garden integrating bridges, water and natural landscapes; and the quiet tea ceremony garden enclosed by bamboo or tree fences.

Zen Garden

The Zen garden pursues the ultimate spiritual state of "cleanliness, emptiness and nothingness," and is an art widely acclaimed by the public. In a Zen garden, natural elements are always static and their color never changes, such as moss, gravel, pebbles, stones and evergreen trees. Flowers are almost non-existent. Elements that are "must-haves" in most other types of gardens, such as shrubs, bridges, islands and water, are also excluded. Only rocks, the sky and earth remain.

Such gardens use extremely simple materials to create wonderfully beautiful scenes, which touch people's souls and give them unlimited room for imagination. They represent a sophisticated philosophy originating from the Zen Buddhist tradition.

In a typical Japanese Zen garden, the selection and layout of rocks is paramount. Rocks with personality, such as granite, limestone and lava, are frequent choices. The number of rocks is generally limited to single digits. Three or five rocks are grouped together with attention to the mixture of different sizes, to create a lively and integrated rhythm. As rocks feature irregular shapes, efforts must be made to stress the resonance and compatibility between rocks, so that their arrangement goes hand in hand with the overall environment.

Here is a picture of one corner of a Chinese-Japanese joint venture, designed and built by the author. In a Japanese garden, the stone lantern, fences and gravel in the waterless stream are typical components.

The use of gravel is highly indicative of a Zen garden. Fine sand stones or gravel with a diameter of six to seven millimeters are selected. The ideal colors are light gray and light grayish white. There are specific symbolic meanings attached to the different layouts: straight lines represent quiet water; small waves stand for slow-flowing streams; large waves represent rushing currents. The materials appear in a diverse range of water styles, including bamboo bar, curve, whirlpool, flower, sea wave and pane, which create the stylish beauty of dry streams.

Stroll Garden

A stroll garden is normally huge, covering an area above three to four hectares. It contains all the elements of a typical Japanese garden: hills, garden paths, islands, ponds, streams, bridges, stone lanterns and water bowls, and bamboo fences. Usually a big water surface with irregular revetments and isles is the main part of this kind of garden. Stepping stones are made into zigzag paths to bring

In the Japanese garden, the bowl for washing hands is usually placed in the master's room or in a low corridor, porch or outdoor yard. It is often made of large, natural stones. They come in a variety of shapes, each bringing with it simple beauty.

fun of walking in the garden. To build such a garden, techniques used in Chinese classic gardens, including "view borrowing" and "view leaking" are often implemented in the layout.

A rich variety of plants are grown in a stroll garden. They include maple trees, whose trunk is small and growth is slow; beautiful five-needle pine trees; small trees featuring diversified shapes; a mass of shrubs; groundcover plants that grow on rocks; Buddhist pines; hemlocks; and azaleas. Evergreen plants are found everywhere, serving to present a vibrant garden landscape at all times, and provide a green backdrop for brightly-colored flowers or plants.

Drawing upon features of Zen and tea ceremony gardens, the stroll garden integrates year-round landscapes with a tranquil and natural country air. Its quietness and depth is intriguing, boasting natural and wild pleasure often lacking in Chinese gardens. At the heart of its attraction is the uniform combination of plants,

surrounding environment and overall landscape, which transforms into a low-key natural beauty, and deserves quiet appreciation and deep thinking.

Tea Ceremony Garden

The tea ceremony garden is more recent category of garden developed by tea ceremony ancestors. A tea ceremony garden is often named after the owner of the tea house. Such a garden is normally located in a forest, designed primarily as a rest area for visitors.

Many "trump stones" are placed there to indicate that visitors should abandon all conventional customs and distracting thoughts, and instead focus on their inner souls. A stone hand basin is one of the typical garden elements. With a primitive and unfinished texture, it is often put in the shade, and used both for body cleaning and tooth brushing. There are two types of hand basin—the squat type, commonly used in a tea ceremony garden, and the upright type, one meter in height and commonly placed in a corridor or gallery.

Stone lanterns are must-have elements in Buddhist temples and Japanese gardens. Hundreds of lantern designs are available, and they are featured in tea ceremony gardens to provide light. A stone lantern is often named after the owner of the garden. The appreciation of stone lanterns in a garden reminds people of their simple and unsophisticated beauty.

While the classic Chinese garden is normally split by walls, artificial hills and plants, in Japanese gardens, plant fences are most frequently used. Featuring diversified shapes, they can be made from bamboo branches or joints, bark, woven strips, shrub trunks and tree branches. Thanks to such fences, the garden can be assured of privacy and harmony with nature. Bamboo is widely applied to other aspects of a tea ceremony garden, such as bamboo curtains, water channels and key canisters. Bamboo plays an irreplaceable role even in an area as small as one to two square meters.

Gardens in southern China are usually private ones, often scattered in the alleys of towns. They take up little space, but despite their small size, they contain grand scenery, with each step bringing you to a new scenic spot. This helps to illustrate the charm of these gardens.

Four Necessary Elements in Creating a Chinese-style Garden

1) Landscaping with Stone

The vast country of China is home to versatile and colorful natural landscapes, including numerous famous mountains with quite different appearances. Gardens that aim to recreate natural landscapes regard mountains as the key element. Therefore, at a private garden with limited space, using stone to represent mountains becomes the first priority. The successful invocation of a mountain in a garden decides whether the replication of nature, and the garden itself, achieves success.

Mountains built in a Chinese garden apply earth, stones or both, to varying degrees. But in southern gardens, most garden mountains, small ones in particular, are made of stones. They can be divided into three types according to size and location—mountains that spread across the garden, compound mountains, and independent peaks. All stones used in mountain making are carefully selected and graded according to the four-letter standard—"thin, leaky, thorough, wrinkled." In addition to carefully selecting stones, a series of landscaping techniques must be applied to create artificial hills with unique styles, beautiful exteriors and a backdrop on each side. As a result, the enjoyment brought about by mountains in nature is in vivid display within the garden.

There are eight expression methods in stacking artificial hills: garden hills, hall hills, tower hills, pavilion hills, pond hills, study hills, cliff hills and indoor hills. Involved landscaping techniques include

The design of a Chinese garden should suit the geographical conditions. When building scenery of heaped stones, you should pay attention to whether the stones are concave or convex, leaky or solid, wrinkled or smooth, and high or low. Natural stones matched with appropriate plants bring greenness and a special quality to a garden.

embedding cliffs, turning stones into a feature, creating a hill formed by a single stone, artificial hill stacking on dry land, year-round artificial hills, and building a hill adjacent to water. Each technique has its own characteristics, while all share common features. Top choices for stones are the famous stones from Tai Lake in Jiangsu Province, yellow brownish stones, Lingbi stones from Anhui Province, Melaleuca stones and Xikeng stones, among others.

Artificial hills should be built by following the artistic conception of natural mountains. There are traditionally "Ten Must-haves," "Six Taboos" and "Four Must-not-haves." The "Ten Must-haves" are: hierarchy, layers, undulations, twists and turns, unevenness, unity, coherence, order, balance, and a blend of fantasy and realism. The "Six Taboos" state that stone hills should not resemble censers and candles, a pen stand or a vase, sabers and swords, an iron fortress, a castle fortress, or a rat hole or an ant hill. The "Four Must-not-haves" are: dyed stones, messy stone textures, an orderly distribution of stones, or many gaps between the stones.

2) Landscaping with Water

Water is the second essential element in building a Chinese garden, and private, temple, natural and royal gardens all feature water. The design of water landscapes depends on circumstances. Based on the size and layout of the garden itself, water either flows in turns and twists, or swirls around in a deep and tranquil manner, realizing the organic fusion of stones, plants, buildings, fish and flowing water.

Chinese gardens have always taken the construction of water landscapes seriously. Despite its small area, every private garden has water. The structure of water landscapes varies according to conditions. Designers of private gardens may choose to make use of an existing low-lying area, or dig a new pond. But most water is static, expressing a tranquil, stable, deep and clean beauty.

Water is also common in temple gardens. Almost every temple has a fresh water pond, which caters to the needs of local residents and tourists. Such ponds are either derived from natural spring sources or developed from downstream spring water. As temple gardens are located in the wild, with free access to flowing water, their water landscape tends to be dynamic and active.

Among natural gardens, the West Lake in Hangzhou is globally famous for its water landscape. The silhouettes of weeping willow trees reflect on the rippling water, giving tourists a unique view with each step. The organic combination of man-made islands and natural views brings out the best in each. Thanks to this artistry, the West Lake is the crown jewel of water landscaping in Chinese natural gardens.

Royal gardens have borrowed the distinct natural features of southern gardens in water landscaping. The Summer Palace used to be called the Garden of Clear Ripples. Its renovation copied the composition of the West Lake, to create a masterpiece of water landscaping, which is tranquil, deep and filled with the wild enjoyment of the mountains.

Three things are crucial to water landscaping in Chinese gardens. Firstly, the design should take advantage of reflections on the water, such as the blue sky, white clouds and elegant pavilions. The water becomes colorful and delightful because of them. Secondly, clear water lays the foundation for creating features with animals, especially fish. Thirdly, growing aquatic plants in water adds a colorful and bright twist to the water landscape. Such plants include the lotus flower, pond lily, water caltrop, wild rice stem, reed and fleur-de-lis. The lotus flower has long been a particular favorite in private gardens.

While the artistry of water landscaping varies in different types of gardens, royal, temple, natural and private gardens do share the following points in common.

Water used in gardens must be flowing, even if the surface may be static. To make water flow, its source is essential. A flowing water source is the lifeline of water landscaping in gardens. Royal, natural and temple gardens usually get their water from rivers or streams. Ground water is plentiful in southern China, so many private gardens link water inside them with outside rivers, or dig wells to replenish water continuously.

The water landscape in gardens must feature twists and turns to appeal to visitors. In order to achieve such visual effects, the first priority is that "the source has to be hidden." In other words, special treatment should be adopted to hide the water source either in a cave or in a stone gap. Secondly, efforts should be made to "divert the flow" so that water spreads across the garden in twists and turns, thus highlighting the core features. Thirdly, one should use the technique of "converging and disseminating." In other words, the water surface can be divided by curvy banks and bridge corridors to create the effect of water merging together and splitting apart.

The water in gardens can be separated by white walls, corridors and even bridges and banks. Thus, multiple layers are formed to enrich the visual effect of landscape. If water is abundant, artificial

Water can bring a sense of delight to a private garden, even in a small space. A waterfall adds a dynamic quality, doing away with silence and stillness. Water creates clear ponds and winding streams that stimulate our imagination and bring life to the garden.

Yu Garden is located in the old part of Shanghai. It covers around 30 *mu*. Within the garden, mountain rocks are ingeniously heaped, reminding one of the scenery of faraway mountains and caves. The flowing water and overlapping flowers and trees make the garden vibrant and alive in all seasons. Yu Garden is one of the most classic gardens in southern China.

islands of various sizes and shapes can be constructed to add more features to the landscape.

As gardens are always tranquil and graceful, all kinds of sounds produced by man-made waterfalls or springs can provide a pleasing acoustic element that adds to the beauty of the landscape. The sound of water may set off the tranquility of the surroundings, and at the same time introduce a musical element to the space.

Colors of nature are diversified and unpredictable. Water itself is clear and plain but has the potential to adopt versatile color changes. If mixed and matched properly with surrounding areas, water can help create rich and colorful visual esthetics. Water plays two functions— "enlivening" and "borrowing." The former means that

its clean and neat color breaks the depth of surroundings and gives the garden a lively feel; the latter refers to its reflecting the colors of surrounding buildings and plants, generating ever-changing beautiful colors on the water surface.

With seamless integration, water landscape and buildings set each other off and are mutually complementary. There are three common designs—water landscapes surrounding a building complex, a complex surrounding water, or buildings interspersed with water scenes. In handling the relationship between buildings and water, garden designers must conform to local conditions. Large gardens should be on water, while small ones should be near a water source. The height of the water level determines the esthetic effects of the landscape.

Here is a picture of the Rainbow Corridor in Humble Administrator's Garden, Suzhou. The corridor links together various buildings in the garden, dividing the space and enriching the scenery.

3) Landscaping with Buildings

Buildings are the third necessary element in Chinese gardens. Their relationship with the garden landscape should be one of perfect harmony and congeniality. Their exquisite and appealing style makes gardens even more attractive in the eyes of beholders.

Apart from meeting the practical needs of visitors—for example, protecting them from rain and excessive sunlight, and giving them a place to rest—garden buildings must be combined with surrounding environment and plants in an organic manner. They feature diversified varieties, with the most common designs being pavilions, corridors, stone boats, halls, kiosks, waterside pavilions, rooms, lofts, Chinese belvederes, towers, bridges, roads, garden doors, cave doors and carved windows.

In Chinese gardens, ancient buildings have distinctive color schemes. For example, the floor may feature green stones, colored stones or red bricks. The terrace may feature white jade. Wood rails may feature red paint. Walls may be painted yellow, gray or white jade. In addition, there may be colored beams, girders with drawings, red pillars, colored glass eave tiles, and ridges.

The color of garden buildings is determined by the garden's nature and scale. Southern gardens are mostly privately-owned and built for study and personal reflection. They are therefore designed to be quiet, relaxing and recreational. Colors are mainly unsophisticated and light. A cold and plain palette is chosen, reflected in the white walls and black tiles, but certain bright colors are used occasionally

Various combinations of the pavilion, corridor and veranda in gardens in southern China enrich the view. Components of different heights are interwoven with the natural environment, making the garden attractive to visitors.

on porches, halls, couplets or steles to add a lively touch. The natural environment of green mountains, clear waters, small bridges and flowing streams may be complemented by garden buildings featuring white walls and black tiles. As a result, the garden invokes a quietly elegant and simple touch.

On the other hand, due to the cold and dry weather of northern China, a warm and bright color palette is used for garden buildings there. The strong green and red contrast sharply and have a heavier presence. Buildings inside a royal garden favor a warm palette to generate contrasting visual effects. The abundant use of yellow roofs, bright red walls and doors, gold ornaments, and colorful paintings hung above Chinese brackets and girders, composes a magnificent and classic royal style. Buildings in temple gardens apply a mostly yellow palette, followed by bright red.

4) Landscaping with Plants

The fourth necessary element in making a Chinese garden is the careful selection and use of plants. They not only provide essential layering in a garden but also help split the garden into different zones and vary the height of the topography. Some plants are selected primarily for the admiration of their flowers, while others for their leaves. Plants may be chosen and arranged according to people's tastes, and may sometimes appear random, but an in-depth significance lurks behind the apparent randomness. The design of plants is an integral part of the design of gardens. The density and height of plants, as well as the relationship between flowers and trees, provides flexibility in using the space within gardens.

Plants used in Chinese gardens have diversified varieties based on different methods of categorization. If based on usage, they can be categorized as flowerbed plants, hedge plants, groundcover plants, sunshade plants, climbing plants, street plants and bonsai plants. Plants can also be categorized based on climate as tropical plants, sub-tropical plants, cold-zone plants, desert plants and plateau plants.

They can also be divided into herb plants and woody plants. The former includes three types—annual and biennial flowers, perennial flowers, and those with flower bulbs. Most annual and biennial flowers are bred through seeds, blossoming in the spring and withering in the same year. Those that blossom in the following year are biennial flowers, suitable for adorning flowerbeds. Perennial flowers, also known as flowers with perennial roots, can keep growing for years. They often wither in the first half of winter and grow again in the next spring. In warm regions, they may blossom all year round. Flower bulbs feature fat modified stems or roots, in the shape of a lump or bulb. Common bulb plants include lilies and gladiolas.

China boasts a rich diversity of woody plants, including needle-leaved trees and shrubs, and broad-leaved trees, shrubs and lianas. Needle-leaved trees are tall, straight and beautiful, and include these famous types: cedar, monkey puzzle, umbrella pine, giant redwood and golden larch. Deciduous needle-leaved trees, such as golden larch, grow fast and change when fall comes. Evergreen needle-leaved trees have leaves that never wither. Needle-leaved shrubs such as pine, cypress and cedar are inherently short. As they are creepers, they can be used in hedges, or for decorating roadsides and corners. Some coniferous trees are also inherently short.

Broad-leaved trees include evergreens such as bamboo and magnolia trees. There are also deciduous broad-leaved trees, such as the aspen and elm. Small trees like orange, plum and osmanthus trees are pleasant to look at and their fruits are edible. As a result, they make a perfect plant in gardens. Broad-leaved plants are short and well within people's eye level, enhancing the garden vista. Their leaves, fruits and flowers are perfect for being admired by visitors. Common examples include rosebay, flowering plum and weeping forsythia. They may be planted in the garden as individuals, in groups, or mixed with trees of other types. Broad-leaved lianas are

Tunnel doors and carved windows are unique to classical Chinese gardens. Windows and doors embedded in a wall often become a frame through which one can enjoy the view beyond, as if appreciating a vivid picture. They help to combine different spaces and build up the layers of scenery.

mostly grown as climbing or green plants. Wisteria, Chinese trumpet creeper and Boston ivy can cling to walls or stands. Evergreen lianas such as kyphosis bamboo, ivy, and star jasmine boast distinctive demeanors, and are therefore commonly used in gardens.

Each plant in a garden has its own physical beauty, which can be divided into five parts from an esthetic point of view, namely: color, posture, scent, sound and light. Color is the first factor to consider in selecting plants, as it easily arouses people's attention, triggering a strong visual excitement. Green is a mild and comfortable color, giving a sense of vitality as well as calmness, tranquility and coolness. Colors of plants are prone to changes, as they vary according to the four seasons. Thanks to multi-colored, beautiful flowers and leaves, an ever-changing, poetic ambience is created.

Plants across the world feature different bearings and postures, but each has its own natural beauty. Take the commonly-seen pine tree as an example. It does not produce any flowers or fruit but has

a proud, elegant style and charm. Pine trees can be seen as having various types of attractive postures, characterized as lying, looking up or bowing. When choosing a plant, special attention must be paid to selecting luxuriant but well-spaced branches and leaves. This produces different visual effects from varying distances.

All in all, there should be a pursuit of "distinctiveness, sophistication and elegance." The design of plants should focus on simplicity instead of fussiness. In addition, the designer should adhere to the artistic standard of a flower in every month and a different scene in each season.

There are numerous scented plants in nature, such as osmanthus, winter sweet, gardenia, jasmine and orchid. Each has a distinct fragrance and period of florescence. Osmanthus trees are evergreen, and once autumn comes, the scent of their flowers is strong with a sweet tinge. On the other hand, the scent of the orchid is light but deep and often comes out after a frost. The scent of plants can bring

Decoration is important to Chinese gardens. On the surface of a large blank wall, you can grow one or two climbing plants. The contrast between green and white drives away dullness and brings vitality to the wall.

joy to people both mentally and physically, making them feel both healthy and excited.

Plants grow in natural environments, so they are struck by winds, storms and snows, producing various sounds. Some sounds are light and soothing; some are like music from heaven; yet others are strong and powerful. As a result, various musical "flavors" are created. To add this musical dimension to the garden, trees with leaves that produce sound when being struck by winds and storms should be favored. In addition, the quantity of plants should be taken in account, in order to create the best acoustic effects.

Plants are beautiful and charming. The light effects caused when mixing them with sunlight, moonlight, water and candlelight can create a breathtaking scene. The reflections of lotus flowers, reeds, red flowers, and green trees are intoxicatingly beautiful. Thanks to the light, layers of the landscape are further enriched. Be it in a dynamic or static state, the visual space is expanded due to careful selection and design using plants.

Chapter One

The Layout of Chinese-style Gardens

Garden design is indeed an art, but it is also should be functional and adapt to the needs of users. Therefore, a successful design should encompass both esthetic and practical values. A checklist must be prepared, and a theme must be decided on ahead of time. The checklist must include all elements required of a garden, such as stones, water, buildings and plants. Normally one garden has a single theme, which must be original, novel and have personality. The design must be conceptualized not only according to functional needs but must also consider local conditions. A one-of-a-kind design concept is crucial to the success of a newly-built garden. One must fully investigate the site to understand its weaknesses and strengths, subjective and objective conditions (area, geography and size of investment), and how to select plants to be grown in specific conditions and locations.

There are several types of garden design—round-shaped tour style, free style, loop-shaped centripetal style, inside-out style, and converging inward style. In planning the garden, special attention should be paid to establishing clear priorities, and varying relations between dense and scarce, positive and negative, curvy and straight, and high and low. Plants and buildings should be mixed and matched in a rational manner, to add color and endless charm to the garden. Let's take a walk in our minds through the following examples of different layouts. Then we can see how all of these elements come into play in designing the most beautiful and balanced garden.

L Shape

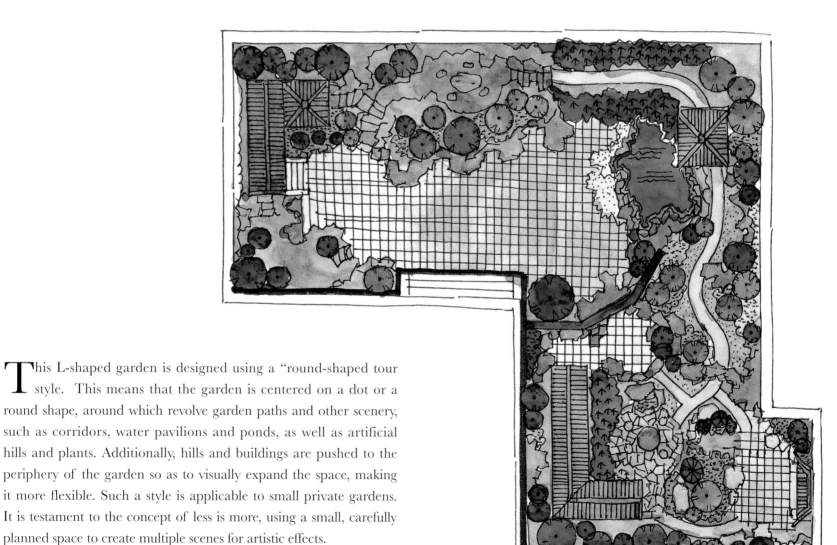

L-shaped Plan

This L-shaped garden is designed using a "round-shaped tour style." This means that the garden is centered on a dot or a round shape, around which revolve garden paths and other scenery, such as corridors, water pavilions and ponds, as well as artificial hills and plants. Additionally, hills and buildings are pushed to the periphery of the garden so as to visually expand the space, making it more flexible. Such a style is applicable to small private gardens. It is testament to the concept of less is more, using a small, carefully planned space to create multiple scenes for artistic effects.

Measuring around 350 square meters, this L-shaped garden is comprised of two parts—the northwest and the southeast. In the northwestern part, hills made of stones are the dominant feature,

L-shaped Vertical Plan

while sloping fields and winding corridors prevail in the southeastern part. The main entrance is situated in the southwest, facing artificial hills covered by lush trees. A winding tunnel cave lies to the left side of the entrance. The "Listen-to-the-rain Kiosk" is small but elegant and secluded; the stairs lead you to the peak of the garden—a large artificial hill, which stands at the heart of the northern part. Stone lanes meander along the hill, with lush trees on both sides. There is a platform with a stone stool on the hill. Its natural and unsophisticated style makes it the ideal place for people to chat with each other while sipping tea.

The stairs down the hill point to a small pathway with high bamboo branches on both sides. Take a turn to the south of the pathway and you are confronted by the Ripple Pavilion, built alongside the water. The clear spring rushes down, generating a pleasant sound, and carp can be seen jumping in the pond. Stones are arranged in an orderly and staggered manner. Coupled with flowers and trees, they create a scene pleasing to the eye and touching to the heart. Walking onto the sloping field, you are greeted by beautiful plants, such as osmanthus, red maple, Chinese flowering crabapple, pomegranate, ornithogalum and redbud. The lane made of stones and flowers stretches ahead.

Then, a cave door made of lake stones blocks your vision. Dense willow trees and bright flowers reappear beyond the door. On its left side lies a side door with a simple and ancient but practical style. Chairs may be utilized on both sides. The white wall, the black top and the lake stones pasted to the wall make a harmonious picture. Turning back to the west, you will see chairs and bamboo on one side and a winding corridor on the other. The corridor is linked to the cave door. The wall pasted with lake stones faces the artificial hill. But with a change of angle, another scene is presented to you. The scale is just right, interpreting the concepts of "less is more," "true mingling with false," and "endless change."

❶ Recreational stone stools are normally located beside bamboo-lined roads, flowing streams decorated with lake stones, or in the shadows of ancient trees. They are designed for people to rest, sip tea, and chat, traditionally providing an ideal place for cultivating character and developing temperament.

❷ With regard to the selection and composition of plants, efforts are centered on making branches and leaves luxuriant but well-spaced, and creating an exquisite ambience. Aiming for "distinctiveness, sophistication and elegance," the designer focuses on creating a landscape that can be observed from both afar and near. Artistic attention is paid to the overall visual effect and feeling, rather than on individual plants.

❸ The novel, unconventional semi-pavilion side door is combined with the white wall in an organic way, looking wonderfully coordinated and natural. The integration of architectural features sets off each, giving plenty of scope for imagination.

❹ Against the backdrop of the white wall, the artificial hill is arranged in a staggered way, and small lanes are hidden within the hill. Chinese flowering crabapple, box tree and dwarf lily turf paint a pretty yet lively picture, where the dynamic is combined with the static.

❻ A "blocking view" works to separate different scenic zones, highlighting their relative independence. Coming upon unexpected views adds a pleasant surprise when transitioning between zones. It may be made from architectural components, trees, shrubs, stones, or some combination of them. However, wood is the most economically effective option.

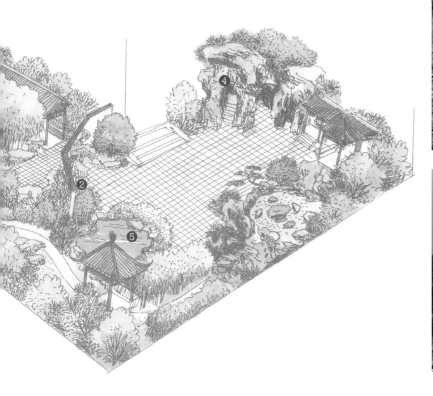

❺ Water landscape in gardens often seeks to add an acoustic component, so that the garden engages all of the visitor's senses. The trickling sound can be complemented by the tranquility of the surrounding environment, and can add a musical note.

Square Shape

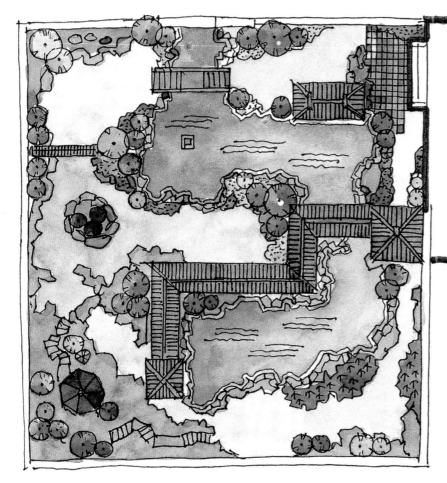

Square-shaped Plan

Despite their small area, Chinese private gardens always take water landscape seriously. This square-shaped garden has an area of 640 square meters, almost one half of which is covered by water. All the buildings are alongside the water. The garden is divided into three parts—the east, the north and the west. The eastern and western parts have a larger area of water. In the north part, the artificial hill pavilion and the corridor shape the main landscape centered on the pond. The pond takes the irregular shape of the Chinese character for concave (凹). The winding corridor links the north with the south, and further splits the water.

Entering from the southeast, you pass a barrier made of trees, and are greeted by the "Yingcui Kiosk," a stone bridge and an inscribed column in the pond. With a good location, the kiosk can become an important feature of the sub-scene within a garden.

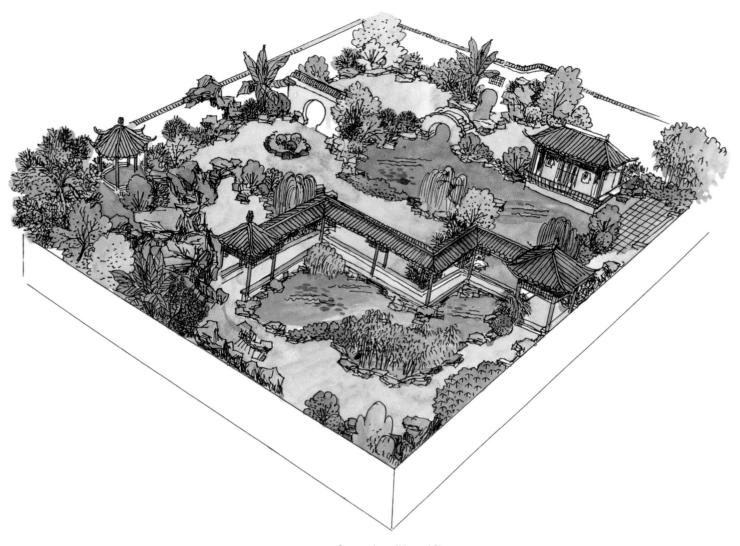

Square-shaped Vertical Plan

Its three sides are clear and open, which is vital to its visual effect. Looking far west, you will be dazzled by a pleasant picture, featuring jagged rocks, zigzagging corridors, lush trees and blooming flowers, such as camphor, osmanthus, Chinese flowering crabapple, arundinaria graminea (Bean) kakino, winter jasmine, winter sweet, peony and azalea. The garden presents a flourishing scene of prosperity all year round.

The garden's northwestern corner is home to its main scenic zone, where the high and steep artificial hill points to the sky, and lake stones extend to the corridor and embankment. The pavilion is the highest point, overlooking the entire garden. A tunnel-like passage is hidden below the hill, which meanders through the garden like a snake. A piece of land on the hill is reserved for visitors to rest. The northwestern part utilizes a "cliff" to hide ugly edges and give

the impression of extra room. The cliff built along the pond appears charming and lively against its reflection in the water.

Walking down the artificial hill, you will see a piece of open land in the southern front. Covered with pebble stones, it sits adjacent to a white wall decorated with lake stones. The layered design, together with the blossoming red maple and Chinese flowering crabapple, enriches the landscape. On the other side is an embankment made of lake stones. Set off by bamboo branches, the small lane is filled with a poetic air. On the left side, you can see a long, narrow, winding corridor, which is central to the overall design of the garden. It cleverly combines two different feelings to make the garden more appealing; standing at the corridor, you are greeted by the artificial hill and plants on one side, and lake stones and plain water on the other.

❶ The staggered whitewashed walls and the round-shaped cave door form a distinctive design element. The garden takes advantage of corridors, carved windows and cave doors, which split space while not completely separating it. As a result, the view is further extended to add to the visitors' enjoyment. Chinese tallow-trees, camphor and magnolias can be planted to enhance the garden.

❷ The hexagonal pavilion is located in the northwestern corner of the main scenic zone, which is comprised of the artificial hill, the rocks and deep hollows. As the highest point, it overlooks the entire garden. Stairs lead to the west and the north. Looking over the southwestern side, one is greeted by a corridor that crosses over the pond. On the eastern side are the pond, bridge, kiosk and lush trees, which are complemented by red maples, osmanthus, camellias, banana shrubs and Chinese flowering crabapple.

❸ Chinese gardens favor varying natural postures and seek a "perfect imbalance." The grouping of Tai Lake stones should be carefully planned to allow smooth placement of the next layer of stones. In addition, these stones should match in terms of texture and edge. A strong emphasis is put on consistency and compatibility between the individual and the whole.

❹ Crossing over the pond, the white "cloud wall" coated with Tai Lake stones features exquisitely carved windows. The lower part is a semi-round cave door, which makes one wonder what may be found behind the cloud wall. The curiosity triggered by just this simple opening is a testament to the "less is more" philosophy found in Chinese gardens.

❼ The central flowerbed is linked to the east of the cloud wall, the south of the corridor, and the west of the large artificial hill. The pleasant views in all four directions are unobstructed. Care is given to the selection and placement of the evergreen box trees, planted on a natural curve. Lake stones are arranged in a staggered but orderly and well-spaced manner; below stand the evergreen dwarf lily turf with boxwood balls in between. Such a layered distribution of different heights makes a natural "mix-and-match."

❺ The construction of the corridor on water is simple, but utilizes a colorful style. Its magic lies in its "curvy silhouette," which bends and twists in just the right places. Such a shape can create views and add a sense of seclusion. The curves allow scenes on either side to penetrate each other, enriching the layers of space. In addition, it provides a place for visitors to rest and appreciate the beautiful views.

❻ A kiosk is generally set up in a quiet, secluded place with an open horizon. When the summer breeze brings out the light scent of lotus flowers, it becomes the ideal location to enjoy the cool air and appreciate the beautiful views. The tall camphor trees, ancient cypress, magnolia trees and gold osmanthus trees grown everywhere create a perfect picture in the autumn. Looking farther to the west, the pond, the lush trees, the mountains and the beautiful pond stones all jump into view.

❽ The corridor is the most ideal tool for splitting garden spaces and scenic zones. A long corridor that stretches across the garden gives visitors an opportunity to realize the beauty of the overall landscape. The use of Tai Lake stones not only brings variety to the layers of the space but also adds enjoyment to the garden.

Rectangular Shape

Rectangular-shaped Plan

This rectangular-shaped garden covers an area of around 2400 square meters, half of which is comprised of water landscape. The whole plan is centered on ponds that appear in irregular shapes. The largest pond is at the heart of the garden. Ponds on both sides are linked by twisting bridges and bridge pavilions, while being split into three parts of varying shapes and sizes. All main buildings are constructed alongside water. At the east stand a single-sided long corridor and an artificial hill, while at the highest point of the garden one can find a hexagonal pavilion. The pavilion overlooks all of the stunning views of the garden.

Walking down the artificial hill, you can see a small pond on the right side of the bridge. When lotus flowers blossom in summer, the pond is lit up by lush green along with contrasting red and white. High up in the lake stones, flowers like winter jasmines, day lilies, snow of June and begonias are planted. Aquatic plants such as irises and reeds are grown along the pond, to enrich the visual interest of the water's surface. The embankment is made of lake stones, in varying heights. Thus, the water landscape is wonderfully appealing. The vastness of the large pond and the narrowness of the small pond produce the artistic effect of shifting from high to low.

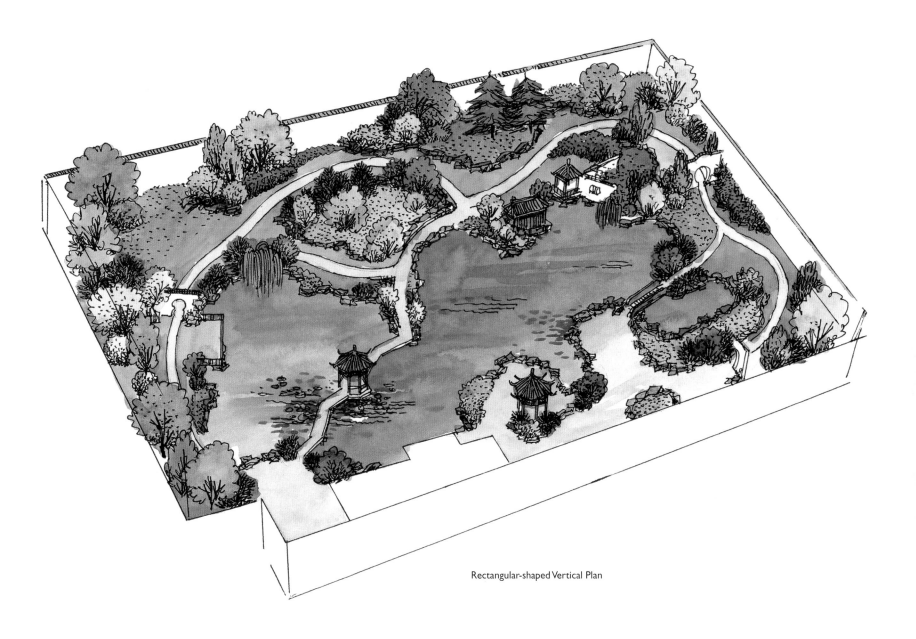

Rectangular-shaped Vertical Plan

Looking at the garden as a whole, you will find that the corridor, kiosk, waterside pavilion, pavilion and bridge line up along the pond. The magic of water landscaping in southern gardens lies in its twists and turns, splitting water into sections of varying prominence and shapes, and allowing it to either scatter or converge. Shapes must not be regular forms of square, round or ellipse. A crooked style is favored over a straight one, so as to create an attractive scenic line. The water can be set off by pavilions, waterside pavilions, kiosks, artificial hills, flowers and trees. The proper insertion of such elements shows off the area of water, while extending its depth. As a result, it creates a lingering feeling of flow, depth and serenity, as well as enhancing the continuity of water.

In a Chinese garden, all elements, including buildings constructed alongside water, and the manipulation of the bodies of water, must appear natural, without any man-made trace. The traditional principle applied here is that "large gardens should be on water while small ones should be near water."

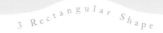

❸ A waterside pavilion is in fact a platform built alongside water, with half of it in water and the other half onshore. The platform is enclosed by rails or a lounge, and therefore enjoys a wide horizon. It is topped by a hip roof with four warped corners. Its accessories are refined and detailed.

❶ The bridge is in fact an overhead road built above water. It marks the crossing of three dimensions—water, land and sky. Bridges in a garden are not there to conquer water, but to draw attention to and embellish natural scenes. They are the icing on the cake for a garden.

❹ Corridors appear in gardens in colorful and versatile forms and layouts. They provide convenience for visitors in times of scorching sunlight or heavy rain or snow. A one-sided corridor faces the main scenery on one side, while it is blocked by walls or other buildings on the other sides, creating a semi-closed visual effect.

❷ The selection and arrangement of flowers and trees should take location seriously. Different geographic conditions, such as hillock, gully, pond and sloping field, require different types of plants, while one must also consider growing conditions, periods of florescence, color and height. In addition, esthetic considerations should be addressed so that each of the selected plants makes a contribution to the whole.

❺ The kiosk is the most common architecture found in a garden. Despite its medium size, it features flexible and diversified forms and styles. Inserted in the natural environment, it forms a reclusive and quiet space of its own, and plays an important role in shaping the landscape of the garden.

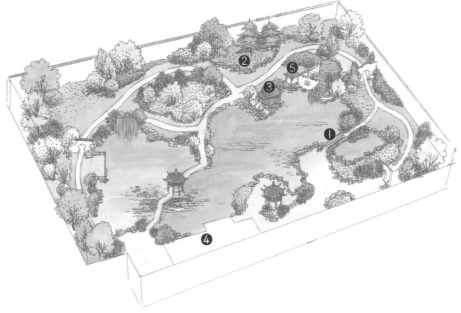

❻ High walls are commonly used in a garden to separate it from the outside world. To add layers to a landscape of a limited space, cave doors can also be applied to separate scenic zones. The most common is the moon gate, which serves not only to direct travel and allow communication, but also is a scenic feature itself.

❼ A hexagonal pavilion may have a single-eave roof, a single-eave pavilion roof or a multiple-eave pavilion roof.

❾ Roads within a Chinese garden feature patterns that reflect natural enjoyment. The patterns may take diversified shapes, including rectangular, trapezoidal and multi-angular forms, as well as organic shapes such as guava, bergamot, bat, flowers, bugs, fish and the traditional Chinese auspicious patterns and symbols of five bats and character *shou* indicating longevity. Polished tiles and pebble stones of varying sizes and colors are materials commonly applied. They are built with meticulous care, with special attention given to the colors.

❽ Cave doors have versatile styles, yet must be wide and high enough to allow people to pass. Typical designs include the square door, two circles, lotus flower petal, *ruyi*, moon window, eight squares and six squares.

53

4

凹 Shape

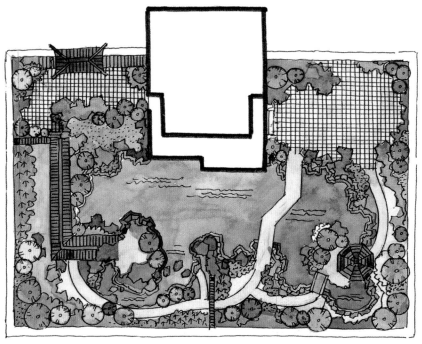

凹-shaped Plan

This garden features a round-shaped tour style, with an area of around 2200 square meters. The garden is divided into four scenic zones—spring, summer, autumn and winter. The summer and autumn zones make up the main landscape, while the spring and winter zones play a supplementary role. Take a walk through half the garden in a clockwise direction and you will be amazed by the scenes of each of the four seasons. Plants and trees are selected according to the season. For example, magnolia, flowering cherry, winter jasmine, camellia and Chinese narcissus are blooming in spring. By including plants that have different periods of florescence, the garden is filled with beautiful flowers and trees all year round. In addition, visitors can experience the scenery associated with all of the seasons.

Entering the garden via its southeastern gate, your eyes are immediately drawn to the foyer made of stacking stones. Lake stones face the gate, with bamboo standing behind. Winter jasmines and azaleas are blooming. Together these paint a splendid spring picture.

The scenery encountered after the foyer creates an abrupt transition. A long corridor stretches forward in a twisting manner. Its surface either stays flat or juts up. Tai Lake stones on both sides are piled up in a staggered manner. The design of plants is layered and distinct, with black bamboo behind and camellia, daphne and winter jasmine up front. Plum, flowering cherry and peach flowers bloom

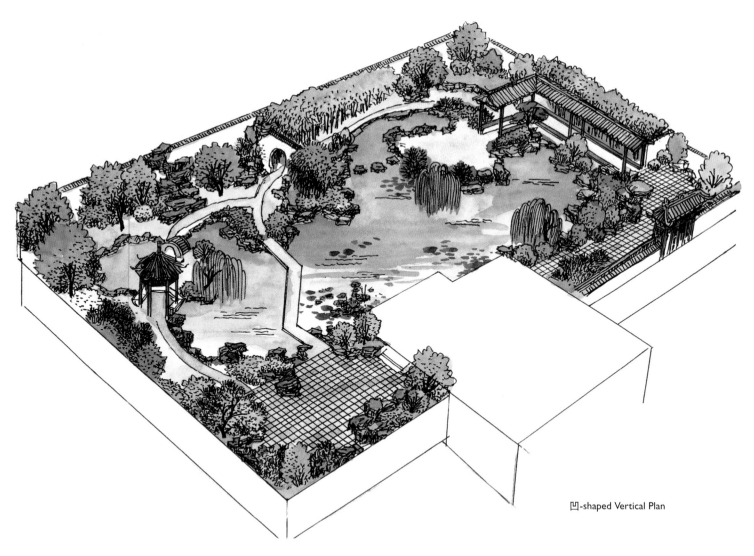

凹-shaped Vertical Plan

together, creating a spring touch. Along a turn of the corridor there appears an artificial hiss cave, which is the "summer" zone, the main scenic area. Lotus flowers are also blossoming in the pond. Their bright color, embellished by pond lilies and reeds, adds more layers to the pond landscape. Magnolia, crape myrtle, pearl blossom and red leaf plums are planted alongside the pond and in corners of the garden, exuding a tranquil ambience.

When you come out of the artificial hill cave, you are already in "autumn" zone. The three-fold bridge on the left side then extends into the "winter" zone. The artificial hill located in the northwest is high, steep and hollow. It sits adjacent to a pond with green, clear and rippling water. The hexagonal pavilion in the center connects the pond's two banks, where lush bamboo and camphor trees stand. The pavilion is a scene in itself, valuable for both esthetic appreciation and practical functionality. The pavilion splits the water into several parts, enhancing the layers of the landscape, while giving people a feeling of flow and serenity.

Red maple and aceraceous plants play a dominant role in the "autumn" zone. Gingko, nectar trees and osmanthus are all typical autumn plants. When autumn comes, the sweet scent of osmanthus flowers fills the air. Such plants are also many people's favorites. Aceraceous plants tend to be bright purple. Thanks to them, this area looks magnificent and stunning with colorful flowers in abundance everywhere.

Located in the southwestern corner, the "winter" zone is home to artificial hills piled up on dry land. Lake stones are pasted to the white walls, and wall corners are enclosed by Tai Lake stones to form flower-beds. Red plum, winter sweet, pelargonium and sophora japonica are planted. When everything withers in winter, a contrasting approach can be utilized by planting the proper amount of pine and bamboo among withered trees and plants. Their wonderful resilience is on full display in the coldest winter.

❶ When pasting lake stones onto the white wall, one must take into consideration the changes in evenness, plainness and height. The semi-relief of lake stones, set off by the white wall and appropriate plants, such as Chinese flowering crabapple, podocarpus and dwarf lily turf, creates an enjoyable green-hued picture. The judicious use of stones generates the effect of "less is more."

❷ One side of the corridor is open while its other side borders other buildings. The separation seems real, but it is in fact not. It can be made into flower-pattern windows, open windows or cave doors. Sometimes several tall bamboos and plantains, coupled with lake stones, create a rather sensational scene.

❸ The pavilion marks the high point of the garden landscape. It strides across the artificial hill, while facing water on two sides and curvy lanes on the other two sides. The hexagonal pavilion is surrounded by plants and stones, well-shaded by green trees. Camphor trees, China firs, hedge bambusa, osmanthus and aucuba japonica set off the water, fish and reflections of flowers on the water's surface.

❹ The artificial hill piled up on dry land faces two sides of walls due to the plain landform. In the limited space, all stones should be piled in a natural manner, taking advantage of their varying sizes and forms, so that no man-made trace is left. Apart from the use of stones, flowers and trees are planted to foster an atmosphere of wild nature, and to enhance the landscape created by the artificial hill. Plants applied include cinnamomum japonica, pittosporum, pelargonium and dwarf lily turf.

❺ Chinese belvederes are very important in a garden. They are large and can be designed and situated in many ways. In a garden, you may find it on a hill, close to a cliff, near water, or even surrounding water. Its style is relaxed and colorful, a perfect embellishment to the natural environment.

❻ Cave doors in a garden feature multiple styles, and have no door frame or window. They have practical and esthetic purposes, allowing for passage between zones while also providing decoration. Looking at scenes through a cave door may produce a focused and framed view. The white wall is complemented by hedge bambusa nearby. Tai Lake stones are pasted to the lower part of the wall, embellished by nandina and sweet-scented honeysuckle.

❼ Chuihuamen (ornamental inner gate having a decorative roof with short carved posts hanging down from the four corners) enjoys a special position in Chinese gardens. Normally it is used as the middle door that splits the courtyard into the front yard and the back yard, which are independent of each other. In addition, linked with corridors, it is capable of physically splitting a garden space, while helping create visual effects such as scene partition, blocking and borrowing. Above all, it creates a view in itself, as a splendid piece of scene-highlighting architecture.

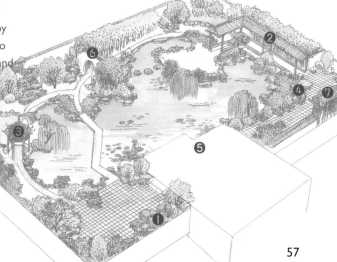

5

T Shape

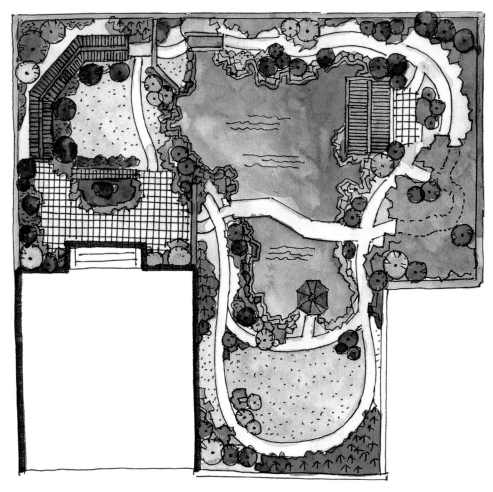

T-shaped Plan

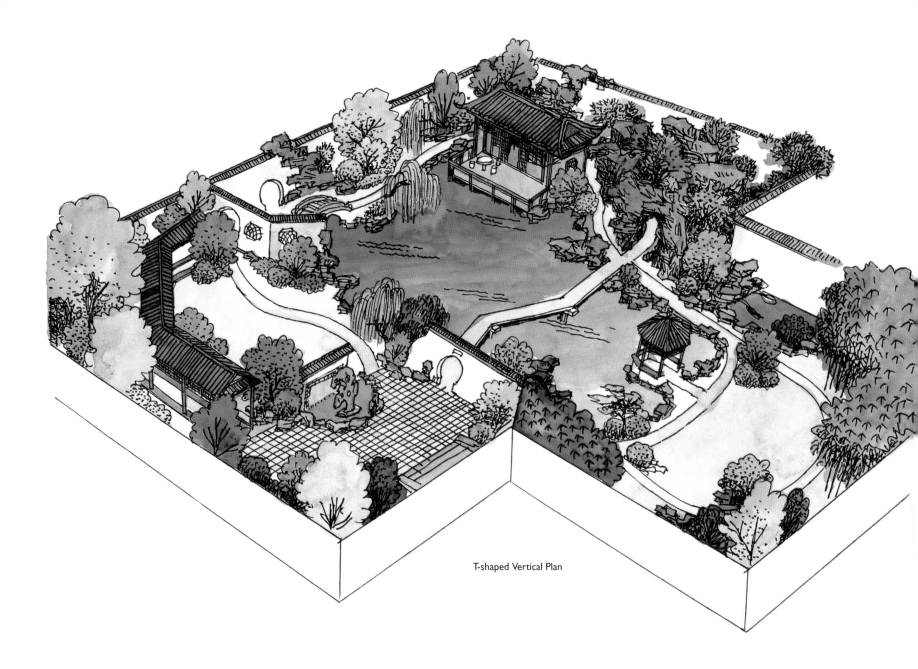

T-shaped Vertical Plan

The saying, "though man-made, still looks natural," sums up the artistry of creating Chinese gardens. The garden shown here is a T-shaped garden comprised of two parts. The west is made up of the open land outside the hall and a leisure corridor, forming the garden's secondary scenery. The main scenery is found in the northeastern part, where there is an artificial hill stacked by stones, along with ponds, kiosks, pavilions, flat bridges and orchards. The orchard itself forms supporting scenery.

The artificial hill situated in the east is the highest point of the garden and overlooks all the breathtaking views across the garden.

The hill is piled up with Tai Lake stones, featuring steep peaks, cliffs and vales. At its bottom are stone houses, stone stools and stone platforms where visitors can rest, enjoy the coolness and sip tea. The pond is enclosed by a circle of Tai Lake stones, whose staggered, twisting and charming style echoes the lakes stones used in the artificial hill, creating a balanced view. A leisure pavilion and a large piece of lawn are situated in the south, which is also home to an open-aired orchard. Fruit trees with various styles, sweet scents and beautiful colors are planted here, including pomegranate, loquat, hawthorn and white jujube.

❶ Walking down the stairs, a screen wall facing the gate jumps into view. The lower part of the wall is enclosed by lake stones to form a flowerbed, at the center of which stands a Tai Lake stone. The white wall and the gray stones make a fascinating picture together. The gaps on the stone and its texture are dynamic and intriguing. Each section features a different style, and each turn brings a new scene. Using a screen wall in this way is termed "view hiding."

❸ Corridors are the skeleton of a garden, and are therefore an indispensable part. The corridor featured here takes twists and turns, while being divided by a piece of wall. The two divided parts are circuitous, while the wall in between has cave windows of all designs. Taking a stroll along the corridor, the visitor can enjoy different views on either side.

❷ On the right side of the stairs stands a goose egg-shaped cave door, embellished by red flowers, such as azalea, against a backdrop of arundinaria graminea. The white walls, black roof, and contrasting red and green plants are complementary. The charming design of the cave door forms a breathtaking framed view, taking in the beautiful pond and stones. Such a technique is called "view blocking."

❹ The artificial hill features winding roads and hollow valleys. The gully roads are designed by combining a sense of reality with fantasy, forming a closed and secluded space to limit the visitor's vision, and enhance the heaviness of the hill. As a result, the desired effect of "the more secretive the scene, the bigger its expanse" is realized.

❺ A group of flowerbeds enclosed by lake stones is set up around the eastern corner. Lake stones are pasted to the whitewashed wall in varying heights. A Chinese flowering crabapple lies at the center of the wall. Against the white wall, lake stones and dwarf lily turf, with ready-to-burst flowers, forms an integral whole with the artificial hill, appearing full of life.

❻ The lake stone artificial hill attached to walls is a common feature of small southern gardens. Using stones to build an artificial hill can seem to expand a limited space. The paper-like white wall attached behind the artificial hill gives the whole scene the impression of a beautiful Chinese brush painting mounted in an exquisite frame. Thus, the perspective is further enhanced, while the artistic mood is strengthened.

❽ The waterside pavilion is always situated close to water, with one side onshore and three sides adjacent to water, creating a feeling of being suspended in the air. The expansive platform extends into the water, rather like walking on the water. The water and the swimming fish form a delightful contrast. It is the ideal place for people to appreciate the beautiful views, read, play instruments, sip tea and chat.

❼ A pavilion is always located at the center of a garden, and therefore enjoys a wide horizon. This pavilion faces a three-fold flat bridge and a waterside pavilion. On its right side lies one of the main scenes of the garden—the big artificial hill. Pavilions alongside water should be positioned low, so as to create a feeling of floating on the water's surface. The lake stones scattered around the pavilion are consistent with the artificial hill. Embellished by camphor, willow trees and wetland plants, this corner emanates a wild, natural air.

6

田 Shape

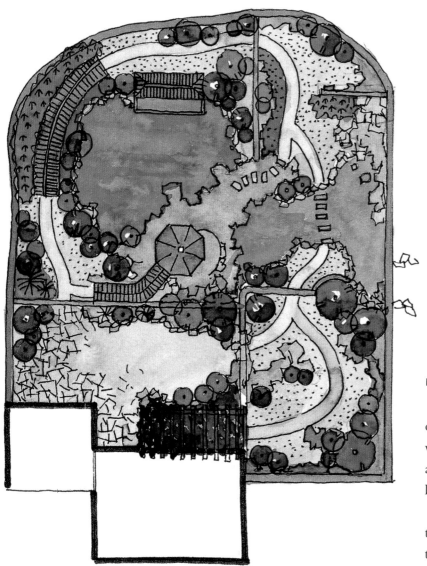

田-shaped Plan

The loop-shaped centripetal style is one of the many patterns of a Chinese garden. As its name suggests, such gardens have a core scenic zone, usually a huge landscape, with other scenery then wrapping around it. It is applicable to royal gardens, which feature an area big enough to contain natural landscapes such as mountains and lakes, and it also can be found in small southern gardens.

The image shown here features a 2000-square-meter garden of this style. Centered on the artificial hill, the climbing corridor and the goldfish pond, its landscape expands in a loop-shaped centripetal structure. The artificial hill, the climbing corridor and the octagonal

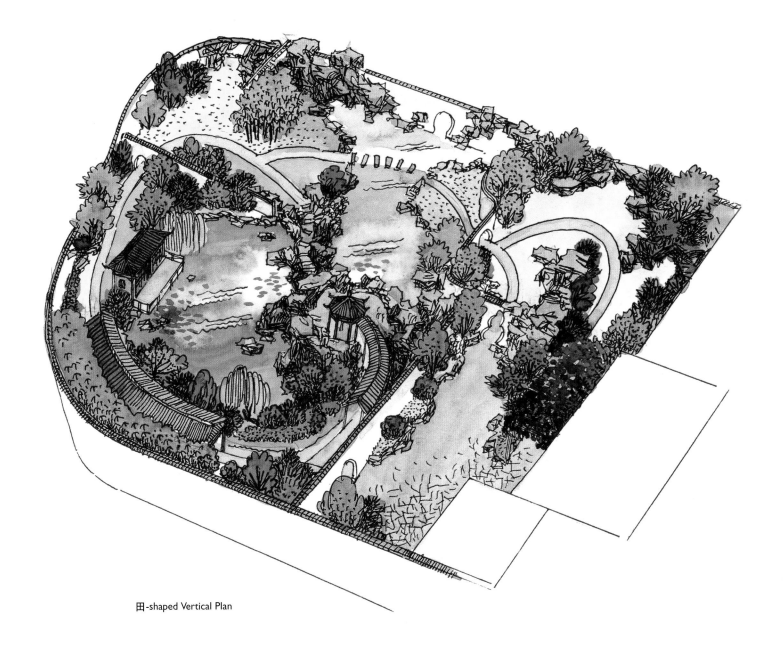

田-shaped Vertical Plan

pavilion form the peak of the garden. You can reach the top of the artificial hill via the climbing corridor to the west. The southern parts of the artificial hill, attached to the wall, stretch into the northeastern corner, while also crossing the goldfish pond. The stairs of the garden road are connected to the northeastern corner. An octagonal pavilion sits on the hilltop, overlooking the views across the garden. The road, which faces the winding corridor to the west, the water kiosk to the north, the waterfall to the east, and the artificial hill cave door and wisteria arbor to the south, gives an impression of diversity and change.

Due to its limited space and high walls, a southern garden can hardly borrow the natural landscapes. Instead, it takes full advantage of internal elements by combining and splitting the limited space into versatile roads and independent scenic zones. Thanks to flower windows, cave doors and framed views on white walls, each scenic zone can connect to the other. The garden landscape is alternately hidden and glimpsed behind various carved windows and framed views. As a result, the multi-angled, multi-orientation and multi-layer visual effects of a "garden inside garden" and "a different view with every step" are realized.

❶ Deciduous liana species such as Chinese wisteria, trumpet creeper, grape and Boston ivy are common in gardens. In particular, Boston ivies can climb independently, while others, such as trumpet creepers and Chinese wisteria, need manual support to grow. These are the most common climbing plants in gardens.

❷ White walls pasted with lake stones are an attractive feature common in southern gardens. Utilizing the limited space, exquisite and transparent stones are put together with lovely bamboo, flowers and trees, making "each inch of the stone filled with emotion." The scene sparkles with wit and humor.

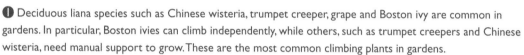

❸ The corridor climbs up the field at a rather steep slope. The stairs are combined with curvy lines. They are of varying heights and lengths, winding upwards with a free, active and tasteful style.

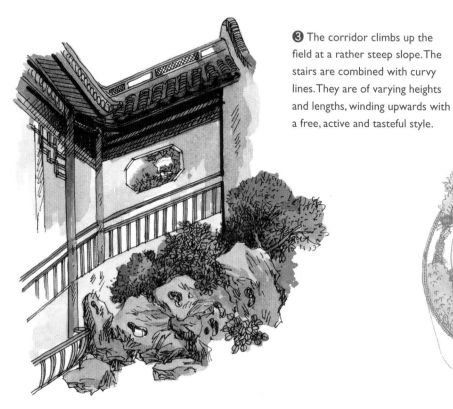

❹ Carved windows, holed windows and cave doors are common decorations in gardens. Views to another zone are visible through the holes in the window, thus separating and joining the space at the same time. As a result, views inside a garden are more lively, diversified, attractive, and full of fun.

❻ Using the artificial hill to conceal the cave door inside the wall may seem haphazard, but it is actually a spectacular choice, as a deep and magical feeling is created. Such an effect, combining reality and fantasy, gives a special kind of artistic beauty to cave doors, carved windows and holed windows.

❺ White walls and black tiles impart a light, simple and elegant tone. The stones of an artificial hill break the monotonous feeling presented by the walls alone, and make a contrast between light and dark. The variety of the lake stones in terms of evenness, plainness and height is lively and interesting, and embellished by plants, it becomes much like a vivid painting.

❼ "View borrowing" refers to the act of using the landscape outside, which includes mountains, waters and buildings of various styles, to enhance the garden's esthetic appeal. The technique aims to combine the "borrowed" outside with the inside, so as to realize the artistic effect of breaking space constraints. This exemplifies the concepts of "less is more" and "seeing the big through the small."

Fan Shape

Fan-shaped Plan

Southern gardens in China are flexible and versatile. The insertion of small gardens forms a close relationship with the surrounding outdoor and indoor space. Such gardens are often centered upon ponds with irregular shapes, so as to make the space inviting, sophisticated and changeable. Thus, a relatively independent, converging inward style takes shape.

This fan-shaped garden attaches great emphasis on water landscape. All main buildings are built around the lake, and their designs conform to the landscape and topography features. The relatively closed, inward garden is centered on the artificial hill pavilions, pond stone boats and bridge pavilions in the southwest, and supplemented by the stele pavilions and corridors in the northeast.

Fan-shaped Vertical Plan

The pavilion on the artificial hill attached to the western wall is the highest point in the garden. One climbs up the hill from the south and goes down to the north. After walking northward along the lane, you are greeted by a pavilion on a bridge. The pavilion is a four-angled, double-eave structure with sturdy and vigorous architecture. It is coherently integrated with the surrounding natural landscape.

Walking further east, you see the northern part of the garden, which is centered on a water landscape. At the heart of the garden, it features a stone boat turning its bow to the south, and its stern to the lake. The stone boat is exquisite and smartly designed. It offers visitors multiple perspectives to appreciate the garden views. At first sight, it looks more like a combination of kiosk, pavilion and tower, but upon closer study, it has the emotional appeal of a pleasure boat.

To the east of the boat lies the corridor with the stele pavilion, which faces a huge lawn in the south, and features a lake behind.

The lawn provides the perfect spot for visitors to appreciate the inscriptions and to sip tea. The whole garden has both closed- and open-air spaces, forming a converging, inward style, where visitors can enjoy serene, quiet and close views.

The selection of flowers and plants follows the principle of "better and less," i.e. focusing on quality over quantity, and employs a style of simple embellishment. Plants are generally grown alone or in groups of two or four. Those grown alone feature the finest scent, color and composure; plants grown in groups appear in the shape of non-equilateral triangles, so that each plant faces a certain direction, for the sake of dynamic and well-spaced planning.

❶ Walls are an important part of garden buildings. There are white-washed walls, abrasive brick walls, "leaking" brick walls, and quarry stone walls. All these walls are full of twists, turns and changes, serving to separate space, and either set off or hide scenery. Green leaves covering the walls create a natural brush painting feel.

❷ Building a pavilion on an artificial hill should take into account the landform, which must be suitable for viewing long distances, the wider the better. Whether taking in a view from the pavilion or looking up at it from the foot of the hill, the pavilion highlights the scenery. With regard to plant selection, Schneider zelkova and ormosia henryi are ideal for venues with high backgrounds, while deciduous trees such as osmanthus, Japan fatsia, banana shrub, red maple and red leaf plum are ideal for venues with a wide horizon.

❸ Tai Lake stones feature versatile styles and rich textures, and the charming characteristics of "thin, leaky, thorough, wrinkled" make them the crown jewels among lake stones. Stone stools and benches scattered along roads and near water must have plain textures for people to sit.

❹ Building a pavilion on a bridge is common in Chinese gardens. While its structure can be diversified—rectangular, square, eight squared, single eave, or double eave— it must be in harmony with the bridge body, as well as the general architectural style of the garden. The bridge pavilion floats above the water, greatly enriching the scenic value of the lake.

❺ In combining views, a variety of techniques can be applied to show off the independent esthetic value of each view in the existing layout. Such techniques include view-blocking, perspective, view addition, objective view, opposite view, leaking-through view, and view borrowing. Tai Lake stones and groupings of trees can split the field of vision and add layers to the landscape; this technique is called "tree blocking."

❻ Views "leaking through" refer to designing carved windows of various patterns on enclosed or corridor walls, so that outside scenes can be glimpsed. There is a rich diversity of patterns, including geometric forms, animals, and in particular, plants. The combination of the real scenes "leaked through" along with the patterned windows allows this artful technique to integrate man-made images with natural scenes.

❼ Doors and windows on a white wall, as well as their frames and patterns, are all versatile and diversified. Their purpose is to transform landscapes into natural pictures. In other words, they are used to frame scenes, creating a landscape "painting" in three dimensions.

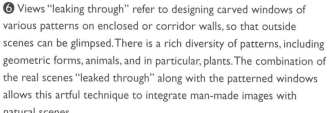

❽ Stone boats often appear in gardens with mountains and abundant water. While similar to a boat, it is not a boat in reality, creating a feeling of surprise and eccentric beauty. As it has the exterior of a boat but not its mobility, it is also known as an "unmoored boat." It has multiple designs, and may have a head without a tail, or conversely, a tail without a head.

❾ Pavilions in Chinese gardens have many varieties and uses. Those that house an upright stone tablet are called stele pavilions. The single-eave square pavilion shown here has winding corridors, goose egg-shaped cave doors, and bottle-shaped windows that are small, elegant and exquisite. The gray windows, white walls, red columns and black roof look steady and noble. The peach trees planted on both sides are set off by Buddha bamboo and the dwarf lily turf-covered floor. The tablet is gracefully hidden behind flowers and trees.

8

Free Style

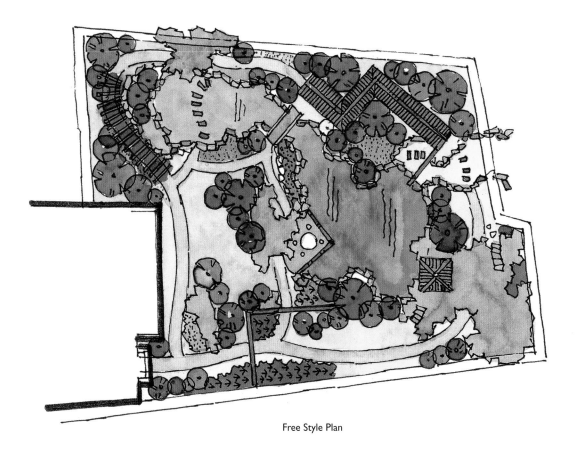

Free Style Plan

Afree style is characterized by acting according to circumstances rather than following a pre-set formula. A flexible design is adopted, whether within a regularly or irregularly shaped area, to incorporate buildings and garden. The use of partitioning, via walls, corridors, cave doors, flower windows and artificial hills, allows different views to penetrate and connect to each other, producing a light and changeable landscape.

This 1200-square-meter, trapezoid-shaped garden is designed in the free, multi-yard style. It is divided into three parts by empty corridors, white walls, artificial hills and arbors. The northeastern part is comprised of artificial hills with a pavilion, tunnels, whitewashed walls and ponds. The northwestern part consists of empty corridors, small bridges, ponds, flowerbeds and waterside platforms. The southwestern part is comprised of arbors, artificial hills attached to walls pasted with yellow stones, stone caves, ponds and stepping stones.

The northeastern corner constitutes the main scenic zone of the

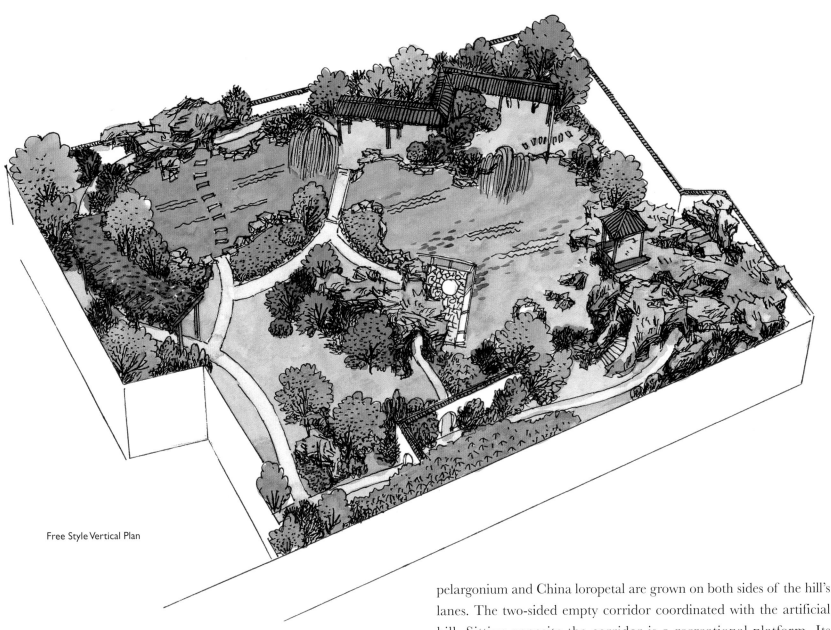

Free Style Vertical Plan

garden. To the northeastern side of the pond lies an artificial hill and banks made of yellow stones. The pavilion on top of the artificial hill is the highest point in the garden. The artificial hill features steep peaks and waterside cliffs. The stones on the hill top are arranged in a staggered and refined way. The garden lane stretching down the hill is circuitous and curvy, while also following the contour of the land. Gold osmanthus, Chinese flowering crabapple, camellia, red maple and camphor are grown around the artificial hill. Plants like pelargonium and China loropetal are grown on both sides of the hill's lanes. The two-sided empty corridor coordinated with the artificial hill. Sitting opposite the corridor is a recreational platform. Its waterside location and wide horizon make it an ideal place for visitors to read, play chess and sip tea. At the southwestern corner, a facade of yellow stones hides the artificial hill's cave door. The methods used include attaching yellow stones to the white wall, or stacking yellow stones to make a cave door on the artificial hill.

Arbors form links among all scenic zones in the garden. The best way for visitors to take a tour of the garden is to follow the arbors. The red flowers and the green leaves attached to the stands give the surroundings a feeling of life and vitality. Water is also an indispensable element, and the aquatic plants, including lotus flowers, pond lilies and reeds grown on the water, make the pond more lively and brisk.

❶ Stepping stones in a garden must be blended coherently with other stones used throughout the garden. If yellow stones are widely used in the garden (for example, in artificial hills or along flowerbeds), they should also be use for the stepping stones to achieve a natural consistency.

❷ One or two weeping willow trees may be planted along the pond. Winter jasmine and primrose jasmine are also excellent choices, or one can grow irises, day lilies and azaleas to create the effect of staggered height. Lotus flowers, pond lilies and reeds can be planted on water, while aquatic plants like reeds can be grown at turns, to enrich the layers of the water landscape.

❸ Inside a garden, to maintain harmony, only one type of stone can serve as the main stone to be widely used in artificial hills, embankments and flowerbeds, without being mixed with other types of stones. In addition, a stone applied solely for decoration should be placed in a prominent location, to enrich the landscape of the garden.

❹ Paths serve to both highlight and create scenery. Garden paths are the means of linking various scenic spots together. They are designed to follow the changing environment and natural landscapes of the garden. They can either bend or curve, providing a natural means of appreciating the views, as well as providing visitors with a relaxing and serene experience.

❺ A waterside recreational platform is a vital architectural element within a garden, allowing visitors to appreciate beautiful views. Its style and nature may be similar to that of the kiosk and waterside pavilion. The difference is that the platform is completely open with an unobstructed horizon. The height of such a platform should not be too tall, as it must be blended perfectly with the water and banks, creating a natural and comfortable feeling.

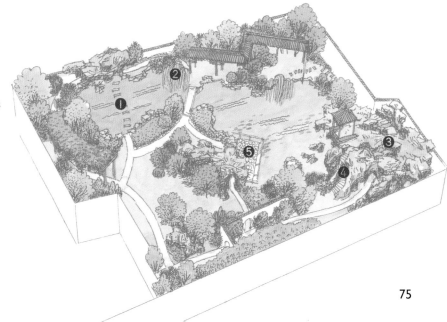

Chapter Two

Stones:
The Spirit of Chinese Gardens

In most Chinese gardens, there are rockeries and stones, which are both poetic and natural. Stone working is part of China's fine traditional culture, and it has a long and rich history. In gardens, stones are presented to reflect spirit and character, so they play a much more important and personal role than a Western visitor might initially imagine. Stones are personified, and their characters are classified as "thin," "leaky," "thorough," "wrinkled," "clear," "stubborn," "ugly" and "clumsy." "Thin" means stones are slender and delicate yet have strength of character. "Leaky" reflects vibrancy and smooth circulation. "Thorough" indicates having a thorough understanding as well as a quick-eared and sharp-eyed temperament. "Wrinkled" means the surface texture of stones undulates. "Clear" means stones are feminine, while "stubborn" means masculine. "Ugly" refers to those with unusual and peculiar appearances. "Clumsy" indicates lack of guile and a down-to-earth quality.

The mountains of gardens consist of artificial rock hills, of which there are two kinds. The first is made up of heaped stones and earth, with the stones usually being Tai Lake stones, yellowish brown stones and Ying stones. The second type consists of an individual standing stone. The beauty of such stones can be appreciated from different angles, and they are mainly Tai Lake stones.

Tai Lake stones come from the limestone at the bottom of the Tai Lake in Jiangsu Province. After many years of wear and corrosion by the lake, stones become fully or partially pierced, and the stones take on a variety of shapes, with many holes and surface wrinkles. The rare and precious stones are those that are thin, wrinkled, leaky and thorough. Tai Lake stones have three colors: grayish white, dark blue and dark yellow. A single, large standing stone can be presented as a rock hill and become the true highlight of a garden. Small ones are often heaped together to be presented as a scenic spot.

In the famous gardens in Suzhou, Shanghai and Yangzhou, rockeries are usually made of Tai Lake stones. The stones are formed after thousands of years of wear, making them hollow, and delicate. They are unique for being "thin, wrinkled, thorough and leaky." Rockeries made of Tai Lake stones best represent the essence of the Chinese garden. Compared with Tai Lake stones, other stones, such as yellowish brown stones, are much smaller; however, they can also be used to create scenery of beauty and charm.

Another type of stone popular for use in the garden is yellow brownish stones made of quartzite, sandstone or grit. They are washed by floods and rivers over many years, and take on a very smooth surface that feels like grease or wax. It is more suitable to pile

Yellowish Brown Stone

Yellowish Brown Stone

Tai Lake Stone

Tai Lake Stone

Lingbi Stone

Huangla Stone

Melaleuca Stone

Melaleuca Stone

them up instead of having them stand singly. If stacked ingeniously, they can present a different style compared with Tai Lake stones.

Ying stones come from the Ying Mountain in Yingde, Guangdong Province. Because of long years of weathering and corrosion, their surface is dotted with dents, fissures and holes. They are ideal material for rockeries. Rockeries may also make use of stalagmites made of green tuff, melaleuca and snow-shaped Xuan stones, made of milky white cubes of quartz vein.

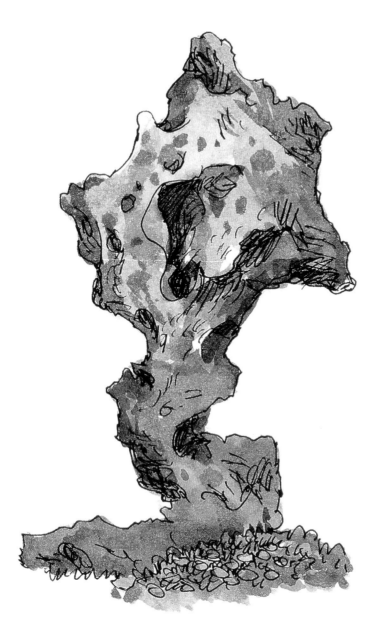

Lingbi Stone

Shaji Stone

Stalactite Stone

Xikeng stones are usually placed in streams or low-lying places. They look round and full and are of varying sizes. Nowadays they are often heaped around a pond near a public lawn. Small Xikeng stones are also used as decorations in private gardens.

Songhua Stone

Xikeng Stone

1

One-stone Hill

The hill made of one stone as an independent esthetic object is very common in the gardens of southern China. The Tai Lake stone that forms a hill must be positioned in certain ways. It can be placed at the gate, and in front of the screen facing the gate. It can also be placed in a flowerbed surrounded by stones or on a lawn, or included in an embankment of stones by a pond.

The gate is an important location because all visitors pass through. Put a stone there, and people can fully enjoy it. Usually only large Tai Lake stones are chosen. Of its four visible sides, the stone's best profile is always chosen, so that its beauty can be fully appreciated. Such a stone can be five to eight meters high, and two to three meters wide. The size depends on the area of the garden. Choosing the right size gives the stone an additional splendor, while an inappropriate size spoils the overall beauty.

In Shanghai's famous Yu Garden, there is a stone called Yu Linglong, which stands alone forming its own hill. It was said to have been intended for a Song dynasty emperor but failed to reach him, and was instead left in Shanghai. It is 5.1 meters high, 2 meters wide and weighs over 5000 kilograms. There are a lot of fissures in the darkish green stone. It is unique, and is the highlight of the garden. Shanghai's Yu Linglong Hill is one of the three most famous of these one-stone hills in southern China. The other two are Ruiyun Hill in Suzhou, Jiangsu Province, and Zhouyun Hill in Hangzhou, Zhejiang Province.

"What is natural is the best": This is the highest standard in evaluating the artistry of a Chinese garden. Rockeries should be built in such a way that they closely resemble real mountains— this is the biggest achievement in terms of building rockeries.

Tai Lake stones are unique to China. Those stones that have been submerged in water are especially valuable. After years of erosion, they become leaky and hollow. Each side of the stones looks delicate and fine. Such stones are rare and much sought after.

A high stone hill, which looks very natural, is situated on the lawn. It looks singular and splendid, surrounded by plantains, geraniums, azaleas and camellias. To its left and right, there are stones that complement the view of the hill. The Tai Lake stone is silhouetted against the whitewashed wall behind it. Together they form a beautiful view. This scene is typical of stone hills in southern Chinese gardens.

When building a rockery on dry land, you can present it as a peak, precipice or cave to make it look grand, aspiring or mysterious. In southern Chinese gardens, you often see a rockery on dry land where the ground is level, and there are no natural mountains or lively water.

Stone hill on a flowerbed. Here are some decorative stones commonly seen in Chinese gardens. Often, one peak is flanked by several stones and set off by green or red plants, creating a vivid image.

At Xiaolian Manor, one garden is encircled by another. The outer garden is centered on a lotus pond surrounded by mountain rocks, a pavilion and bridge railings. In the inner garden, there is a rockery made of lake stones, each of which is only as large as a fist and looks very delicate. There are caves and recesses all around the rockery, which add visual interest and wonder.

There are two types of rockery in Chinese gardens. One is a single, independent peak; the other is made of heaped stones or earth. In gardens in southern China, the single stone peak is appreciated as an independent esthetic object. Since the Tang (AD618–AD907) and Song (AD960–1279) dynasties, the literati have traditionally shown their love for stones and even written works on them. In gardens, stones are imbued with character and spirit, and regarded as a vehicle to convey feelings, wishes and love. That is why you often see single stone rockeries in gardens in southern China.

Beside a pond, one can place delicate lake stones or "stubborn," more masculine, stones as decoration, bringing a feeling of relaxation and entertainment. Stones can produce different artistic effects. It is appropriate to place ancient-looking stones beside plum blossoms, thin stones beside bamboo, and stubborn stones beside plantains. Stones can be placed in rivers, streams, under trees, beside flowers or by a mountainside to create lively images.

The stone hill is usually placed where it can be viewed easily. Entering the gate, you immediately notice the stone hill on the lawn. It is full of fissures, and is thin, wrinkled, leaky and thorough, making it very impressive. In the past, many literati inscribed poems on the stone, thus making the garden famous.

Erecting a stone hill by a lake is also a common practice in gardens in southern China. The stone used to form the hill should be a Tai Lake stone that is intact, wrinkled, thin, leaky and thorough. Tai Lake stones that do not meet these standards can serve as part of the background, and can be placed around the pond, to set off the stone hill.

2

Stone Scenic Spot

The layout of decorative stones is an important element of garden planning. Harmony between stones and buildings, rocks, waters and garden paths can express and emphasize the overall style of the garden. The stones fill open space, decorate the garden and enrich its beauty.

The placement of stones should fit the layout of the garden. They can be put in corners, at the end of a path, or at an intersection. You can place a stone beside bamboo near a wall, or adjacent to plantains against a window. They can also be placed against a tracery wall, at the front of a cave, alongside a small path or plants and vines. Stones can be put in unexpected places to bring additional enjoyment. Decorative stones should be placed at varying heights and at different intervals. They can be dispersed or gathered together. There should be diversity, instead of uniformity or symmetry in the arrangement of stones.

There are many varieties of stones, including Tai Lake stones, stalagmite stones, Xikeng stones, yellowish brown stones, Lingbi stones and Kunshan stones. Tai Lake stones are used most often in gardens, and usually people choose those stones that are delicate, both wrinkled and smooth, leaky and solid, and convex and concave.

Different stones have varying artistic effects. Choosing a fitting variety of stone can help to bring a lively and refined style to a garden. For example, you can put some plantains and maples alongside two or three stalagmite stones. An eccentric arrangement doesn't bring disharmony. Instead, it serves to complement, decorate and beautify a garden.

In small private gardens, heaped stones or rockeries highlight the beauty of natural mountains and water without any trace of artificiality. In these gardens, one experiences many attractive scenic spots, with mountains and forests feeling so close at hand.

Stones and plants each have specific links to the seasons. For example, strong, thin bamboo in the garden can remind one of spring. To bring feelings of summer, delicate and glittering Tai Lake stones can be used to form precipices or cliffs surrounded by clear streams and covered by trees, winding roots and vines.

A set of Tai Lake stones. Tai Lake stones are used most often in gardens. You can gather five to eight stones together to form a flowerbed. They shouldn't be placed at the same height or on the same horizontal line. One or two outstanding stones should be placed in the most prominent and accessible spot, to give people the best view of them. The height of the whitewashed wall behind also determines how you should arrange stones and plants.

Decorative Xikeng stones. Several Xikeng stones can be laid in a creek containing irises, water lilies and other wild water plants. In this way, the division between the bank and water becomes inconspicuous. Here you can see two or three Xikeng stones of different sizes. Above this, China loropetal, winter jasmine flowers and tiger lilies are placed in an orderly pattern. The moving, clear water contrasts with the still objects, creating a poetic picture.

Plants placed outside patterned or carved windows should be those that grow slowly, have a shape doesn't change often, and are handsome. Examples include plantain, black bamboo, hedge bambusa, sago cycad and geranium. If you put Tai Lake stones of different sizes and heights beside them, the image is enhanced, becoming one that is stable and enduring.

Plantain, bamboo, Tai Lake stones. In paintings of ancient Chinese literati, bamboo and plantain appear most often as they are the most poetic and picturesque plants. In Chinese gardens, these plants are two of the most often seen elements, frequently appearing next to lake stones, whitewashed walls or holed windows.

Guyi Garden, one of the most classical gardens, is located in the east of Nanxiang Township in Jiading District, in the northwest of Shanghai. This Ming dynasty (1368–1644) garden occupies around 100 *mu*. In the garden, there are pavilions, kiosks and columns with images of bamboo of various shapes.

In Guyi Garden, there are many peaks made of Tai Lake stones with different appearances. Some are dainty and some are sturdy. Some are delicate and glittering. This represents an essential component of Chinese garden design, namely using objects to convey feelings. There is a saying in China that the wise love water and the benevolent love mountains.

Plants in front of a whitewashed wall should be those that look elegant and have bright colors, such as red maple, red leaf cherry plum, camellia, azalea, nandina or China loropetal. Against the backdrop of the white wall, red flowers and green leaves are like a flickering fire, creating a "soundless poem and a cubic painting" that offers unbound esthetic enjoyment.

Stalagmite stones are often used as decorative stones in gardens. They are slim with a lot of fissures and an uneven surface texture, and their height ranges from one to three meters. Three stalagmite stones placed at varying heights and in different rows can form a very good decoration. They are often placed beside a whitewashed wall, at the corner of a building or outside carved or holed windows. They can also form a scenic spot by themselves. It is particularly wonderful to have two or three stalagmite stones standing on a flowerbed, made of Tai Lake stones, containing both red flowers and green leaves.

Yellowish brown stones, when used as rockery material or as decoration, create a feeling of wilderness and fun. Their color and smooth surface is beautiful. It is delightful to see two or three of them scattered at different heights, accompanied with several sago cycads or azaleas. With the exception of the Tai Lake stones, the yellowish brown stone is most commonly used.

Rockery on Dry Land

The setting up of a rockery on dry land is vital in building a garden. If the pond in a garden can be compared to human blood vessels, the rockery is like the skeleton. The rockery as a self-contained esthetic object is unique to Chinese gardens, and expresses distinct emotions and sentiments. In southern China, a grand and magnificent rockery made of stones is a common site.

There are two kinds of rockery: A single stone can be used to make a hilltop, or earth and stones can be piled up, with large stones placed on the top and sides. There can be different proportions of stones to earth; a small rockery is made up mainly of stones, with the use of a little earth. According to the stacking and size of stones, rockeries can be used for the whole garden, for a certain area of the garden, or as a focal point comprising a single stone. Stones placed in gardens have been carefully selected and processed. Taste in stones decides the artistic value of the rockery.

There are a myriad of ways to heap stones on dry land. They can be arranged in such a way that they look like a mountain, cliff, cave or peak. There are many approaches that can be used quite flexibly. Different stones can be placed together to set each other off and create a complementary feeling.

A basic element of a garden is a rockery that reminds one of mountains and forests. A rockery is not only beautiful, but it also embodies the character and feelings of its designer. Esthetics and sentiment combine in the rockery, where nature is used to represent human characteristics.

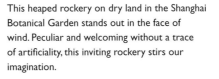

This heaped rockery on dry land in the Shanghai Botanical Garden stands out in the face of wind. Peculiar and welcoming without a trace of artificiality, this inviting rockery stirs our imagination.

91

Stones Embedded in a Wall

Embedding stones in a wall is the most common and economical expression in gardens in southern China. This approach requires very little space, so it is fitting for private gardens, which have limited area and no large-scale natural scenery such as mountains. Stones are embedded in walls to make the garden seem larger than it is, and to enrich the view and complement the trees within the garden.

Embedding stones can be like painting, where the Tai Lake stones serve as the paint and the wall is the empty canvas. The "painting" takes on a three-dimensional quality, because the embedded stones partially jut out, like a relief. Some stones are detached from the wall and supported by lake stones beneath, echoing the embedded stones and presenting a very interesting image.

When arranging stones, there should be variation, creating a natural feeling. You should place them in different areas with different density and height, and use both concave and convex ones. You can accompany stones with black bamboo, arundinaria graminea, plantain, Chinese flowering crabapple, winter sweet, geranium, camellia and azalea, thus creating a poetic feeling. Embedding stones requires garden designers to be highly artistic and capable, so as to create a unique artistic element in a limited space.

In the west of Dianchun Hall in Yu Garden in Shanghai, there is a dragon wall called the Cloud-Penetrating Dragon Wall. The head of the dragon is made of mud, and the scales on the body are made of tiles. The head looks fierce, while the body is curving and winding. The wall resembles auspicious clouds. There is also a reclining dragon, two dragons playing with pearls, and a sleeping dragon in the garden, each of which is quite characteristic.

Embedding rocks in a wall is the most common and simple technique in small gardens in southern China. This placement takes up little space. With a whitewashed wall as the backdrop, rocks are piled in front to form a rockery. This approach creates limitless delight within a limited space.

Chinese garden design often utilizes the concept that a small piece of stone may have many features and personify profound feelings. You can embed rocks in a wall and surround them with lake stones to form a flowerbed, improving the overall look of the garden with this smart arrangement.

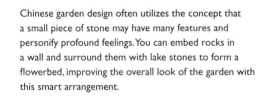

Chinese garden design seeks to create the poetic and picturesque. One way this can be attained is by laying Tai Lake stones against the backdrop of a whitewashed wall, carved window, gate or arch, and accompanying them with plants.

Chapter Three

Architecture:
The Structure of Chinese Gardens

Like stones and water, the garden's architecture is a key element. Rockeries and other stone elements all serve to highlight the beauty of nature, while man-made water features can also look natural. Similarly, with architecture, every thing should look natural and not out of place. In the layout of architecture and the use of space, there is a lot of freedom and flexibility. Bridges, paths, ordinary pavilions, waterside pavilions, corridors and structures on water can all be used. The guiding principle is that the form and spirit of all architecture must be in harmony with the environment, and connect with every part of the garden. In this way, the garden looks natural, serene and reserved, and you just need to walk a few steps to be rewarded with a new scenic spot.

Buildings are essential to the Chinese garden—its beauty is accentuated by the decoration of delicate, elegant and varied buildings inside it. Buildings also help to facilitate visitors' sightseeing. Without suitable buildings, the garden lacks an important element to allow visitors to appreciate the beauty around.

1

Garden Bridge

The bridge in a garden is usually considered as a scenic element. It serves to connect different architecture styles, separate space, and make some scenic spots look distant and deep. The bridge is an important component of the garden and its position makes a significant difference. The bridge has several major functions. First, it determines how you walk through a garden, and can help to regulate passage through the garden. Also, it offers a variety of angles from which to appreciate the garden's beauty. The bridge itself is a scenic spot and serves to complement the water. Finally, it enriches the water view, and separates the water into different areas, some large and some small.

The garden bridge should be placed where it is in harmony with the surrounding environment. The bridge, together with what is in front of and behind it, should form a complete picture. Erecting a bridge at a narrow place is both economical and reasonable. The shape and area of the water determine the layout and look of the

bridge. On a vast expanse of water, there should be a large and tall bridge. On a small area of steady water, there should be a low and small bridge. On a trickling stream, there should be a flat bridge or a winding bridge very close to the water, or stepping stones on the surface of the water.

There are several varieties of bridges in a garden: the flat bridge, winding bridge, pavilion bridge, corridor bridge and arch bridge. The flat bridge is usually seen on a small area of water. It is made of wood and slabs, and can be single-span or multiple-span. As it lies close to the surface of water, the single-span bridge seems to have a particularly intimate connection with the water, and is often used in gardens.

The pavilion bridge has been used in gardens since very early times. You can find shelter from the rain and take a rest in the pavilion. Its size is obviously different from that of the low flat bridge. The tall pavilion bridge has a foundation that looks like the

The Heart of the Lake Pavilion in Guyi Garden in Nanxiang is
located at the center of the garden. A bridge with nine turns lies
across the lake. The pavilion, like a ruby embedded in the center of
the bridge, is a fine scenic spot.

The arch bridge is the most beautiful type of bridge in the garden. Made of stone slabs, the bridge's number of arches is determined by the width of the river. The arch curves are full and round and look dynamic. The variety of number, type and curve of the arches of different bridges brings diverse beauty.

Chinese character " 工 ." It is considered the most beautiful bridge in Chinese gardens.

The corridor bridge is not used as often in gardens. It is usually long, and as its name implies, features a corridor on the bridge. A successful corridor bridge should separate the space around it, enrich the beauty of the water, and make the view behind look very distant, so that the garden looks larger than it actually is.

The winding bridge usually takes two or three turns, although in the most extreme case, it takes nine turns, as in the Yu Garden of Shanghai. The shape of the winding bridge depends on the area of the water. It can be long or short, and with or without railings. Its key feature is that it lies close to the water, so that boats can not pass beneath it.

The arch bridge is one of the most beautiful varieties of bridges. The arch is made of stone slabs or bricks. The number of arches depends on how wide the water is, and can range from one arch to tens of arches. Its shape can be an arc, a semi-circle or two circles. Different shapes show a different beauty of form. In the gardens of southern China, you will usually see semi-circular holed bridges, which look agile and dynamic.

Single-holed bridge. bridges are usually low and simple, and appear light, full and round. It brings special delight when visitors are able to enjoy the view of the stream from a bridge in the small space of a private garden.

Winding bridge with three turns. In limited space, you can erect slabs of different stones across a river to form a bridge. A bridge like this looks simple and poised. It has limited space, and, since it lies near the surface, you feel the water to be close and intimate. In Chinese gardens, bridges are usually very low, allowing only water, not boats, to cross under it.

In Chinese gardens, bridges are often built to divide water into
different sections. The location of the bridge should suit the
surrounding environment. Bridges are often erected where they
can link the various scenes behind and in front of them. In this way,
bridges become a decoration and help to form a completed scene.

Arch bridge made of stones. The arch bridge has many advantages. It employs simple engineering and has a relatively large span. It is not only beautiful but also of great practical use, allowing water, and sometimes even boats, to pass under it. In gardens in southern China, bridges usually have semicircle arches.

Flat bridge. When a bridge and rockery are next to each other, the bridge should be low and short. In this way, set off by the low bridge, the rockery will look even more steep and grand. The straightness of the bridge can also set off the winding of the rockery.

Garden Gate

Yu Garden in Shanghai can be divided into six areas. The inner garden, called the East Garden, covers only an area of two *mu*, half of which is occupied by a rockery. Sunny Snow Hall, Guantao (Wave Watching) Tower, Yanqing Tower and the Unmoored Boat are grouped around the rockery, with flowers and trees intermixed. The layout of the garden is a superb example of ingenuity.

The garden is usually delimited by the wall surrounding it, and people enter the outdoor garden through the gate. A gate may also serve to separate different scenic areas, and give the impression that the garden is larger than it actually is. It can serve as a visual frame, helping to create a vivid and beautiful picture when people stand in the gate and have photos taken.

The gate has two major functions. First, it partitions different scenic spots. A garden must be divided into several sub-gardens, and whitewashed walls are used to separate them. A gate in the wall allows for different sub-gardens to seem connected, physically and visually, keeping the continuity of the garden. Second, the gate brings into view the scenery standing behind it. For example, through the gate, you might see a charming scene of rockeries, bamboos and haw berries, or even pavilions by the water. Thanks to the garden gate, different scenic spots can complement each other and enrich the overall view.

The garden gate comes in a variety of shapes: rectangular, octagonal, gourd-shaped or in the shape of a Han dynasty vase. The garden gate is often surrounded by slate-gray bath bricks, which can resemble a painting frame. The simple and lucid colors look especially elegant and delicate against the white wall. The gate not only enriches the view, but its different shapes can bring their own kind of beauty as well as a sense of fun to the garden.

Circle-shaped gate. In Chinese gardens, the gate in a wall always receives serious consideration. The gate should have an appropriate width and height so that people can easily pass through it, with the height greater than the width. The gate has a frame but no door. It can take on many shapes, including a vase, the moon or a hexagon, with the moon-shaped gate being most common.

Han dynasty vase-shaped gate. The gate connects and merges different areas, physically and visually. Visitors can go through the gate to appreciate the view inside. Windows and gates in a wall also act as frames through which you can take in the scenery beyond, increasing the depth of the view.

Through the beautiful round gate in Shanghai's Yu Garden, you can see the scenery behind, including winding stone railings. By providing this view, the otherwise plain wall and gate are made lively and vibrant, increasing the visitor's sense of delight.

Gourd-shaped gate. While the gate is a decorative element of the garden in its own right, it also enriches the space by achieving the artistic effect of seeing grandeur through something small.

Hexagon-shaped gate. When you casually walk through a gate in a wall and see the scenery beyond, you feel that you are walking into a picture. You begin to focus on that picture and your imagination takes flight. You therefore slow down your steps, spend a longer time in the garden, and feel a heightened sense of enjoyment and peace. This is part of the wonder of Chinese gardens.

Fan-shaped gate. The gate and carved windows in a garden create a "scenery atop scenery" effect, generating a layered view. The space appears deep and profound, and evokes wonderful feelings that can hardly be put into words.

Octagon-shaped gate. Chinese garden design values the winding over the straight, and strives to create an illusory feeling rather than something solid and concrete. However, the illusory should be combined with the real to show the multifold nature of the space. This is one esthetic feature of the gate or carved window—they look as if they are a picture but the scenery beyond is real.

Wall

Dragon Wall

While the wall in a garden is not as essential as a rockery, pavilion or gate, it is still an important part of the overall layout of the garden. The garden in southern China is small and may be crowded with architectural features. To give the impression that there are many gradations of view within a limited space, the wall is used to partition the garden into different scenic spots. In addition, it can serve as a backdrop to set off other scenic features, while also directing the flow of visitors.

In the garden, walls can be adorned in many ways. For example, a straight and plain wall can be turned into a dragon wall, cloud wall, stairway wall, wall with cavities or flat wall. The dragon wall in the Yu Garden of Shanghai is a successful example. The wall is small but still manages to create a grand view. The designer ingeniously built five dragons on the wall, each of which has its own unique features. One dragon seems to be riding on clouds and flying in the sky, while another seems to be reclining and waiting for its chance to fly. There are also two dragons playing with pearls, while the fifth dragon, in the inner garden, has a body made of black tiles and is lying on "white clouds."

In the garden, walls are mostly white with black tiles, and this sharp contrast makes the garden looks simple but elegant. The white wall is a backdrop against which red maple, flowers, grass and rockeries are set off. The effect is that the light and the shadow of the trees are undulating, and the haziness is beautiful. The dull and monotonous wall now becomes lively and fun.

The Dragon Wall in Yu Garden in Shanghai has unique features, including a rhythmic beauty that is traditional to the Chinese people. Five Dragon Walls were ingeniously erected in the garden and each has its own characteristics. Here, on the Cloud-Penetrating Dragon Wall, clouds float below the dragon, which looks as if it is about to raise its head and fly upwards into the sky. The interesting White Dragon, in the inner garden, dissipates the dullness and monotony of the wall and brings great scenic beauty to the garden.

Cloud scroll-pattern decorated wall. In private gardens, walls are used to increase the gradations of view within the garden, to separate scenic areas, or guide visitor traffic. The wall is an important tool in the structuring of space.

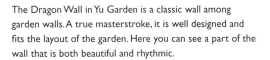

Cloud wall. The wall has many manifestations, such as the cloud wall, stairway wall, wall with cavities and flat wall. It is mainly used to separate space, set off scenery, or screen the visitor's view of certain scenic spots. While a straight, long and solid wall can be quite dull, a skillfully designed wall that suits the environment can bring unexpected effects.

The Dragon Wall in Yu Garden is a classic wall among garden walls. A true masterstroke, it is well designed and fits the layout of the garden. Here you can see a part of the wall that is both beautiful and rhythmic.

Stairway wall. In private gardens in southern China, which are usually small, buildings are relatively dense and separated from the hustle and bustle of busy streets. In the garden, high walls are erected as partitions to increase the layers of view and better use the limited space.

Shadow of the wall on water. Plantains lie near the water and flower wall here, decorating it. Visitors can vaguely see the scenery beyond the round, whitewashed wall mirrored in the pond. This effect increases the layers of scenery and brings a lingering enjoyment.

4

Carved and Holed Window

In the garden, carved and holed windows—those featuring a decorative pattern screen of some sort rather than a clear, single opening—can have many shapes, and can be horizontal or vertical. When glimpsed through such a window, which provides partial screening, the scenery seems multi-layered, and the changing effects of light are accentuated.

The design of carved and holed windows depends on the surrounding environment. The window takes on one of two kinds of shapes: geometric or natural. The traditional geometric shapes commonly used are the swastika (a common Buddhist symbol), ice crackles, fish scales, lines and *ruyi*, a Chinese jade ornament. The natural shapes are mainly those of flowers, such as plum, orchid, bamboo, chrysanthemum, lotus, tropical citron with finger-shaped fruit, and pomegranate. Also, animal shapes such as the lion, tiger, dragon-shaped cloud, phoenix and crane are common. There is often

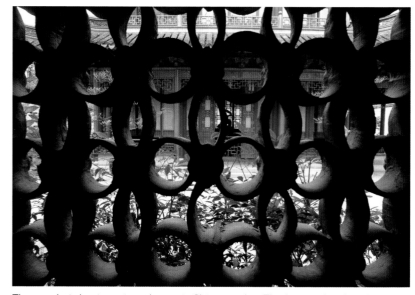

The carved window is a unique element in Chinese gardens. The design makes the otherwise dull and monotonous wall instantly vibrant and lively, thanks to the scenery seen through the perforations.

a continuous row of windows in a wall. If their shapes are different, they are called a miscellany of windows.

Patterns in the carved part of the window are usually made of tiles, thin bricks or wood. There may also be patterns of human beings, mountains, rivers, flowers, trees or animals that are created using a steel wire skeleton covered by hemp or plaster.

Carved and holed windows are used frequently with great skill, enriching the view of the garden. Patterns are seen in the holed parts of the window, altering and enhancing the scenery. Also through carved windows, which are scenic features in themselves, you can see other scenic spots. Carved windows give wings to our imagination. Sometimes you inadvertently see the scenery outside the window, and feel that it is indistinct—partly hidden and partly visible. The window brings gradations to the view of the garden.

Flower-pattern window. The carved window adds a sense of the dynamic to a solid wall. It separates space and makes the scenery beyond partly visible. The delicate perforations can be round, hexagonal or organic in shape. The flower-shaped perforations in the Suzhou Gardens are especially beautiful.

Wooden carved window, for long corridors and whitewashed walls

Wooden carved window, mainly for spacious halls

Wooden carved window, for secluded and serene verandas and buildings

Grey brick and carved window, for long corridors, verandas and buildings

The carved window can screen off or usher in scenery. Ushering in scenery is the more important function. Through the carved window, you can see a rockery or slim bamboo shoots. The window also brings into view mountains both far and near, as well as buildings. The effect is like a traditional Chinese painting. Here you can see blooming purple magnolia through a carved window in Guyi Garden in Nanxiang.

Flower-pattern window made of four semi-circles, mainly for whitewashed walls and long corridors

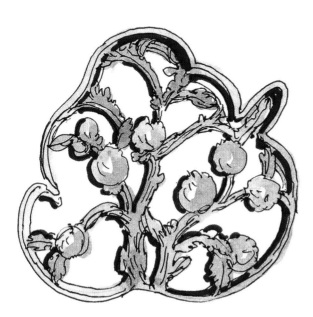

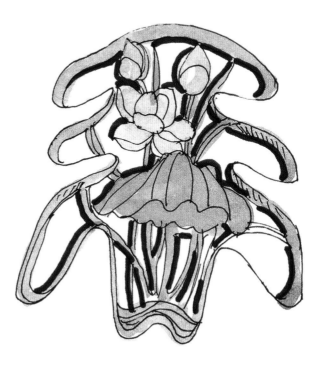

Flower-pattern peach-shaped window, for whitewashed walls, long corridors and courtyards

Bonsai-style window with a pond lily pattern, for whitewashed walls, verandas and corridors

Pavilion

Hexagonal Pavilion near Water with Young Water Lilies

In a garden, the pavilion is often located at the top of the hill, by the water, on the side of the road, or within a grouping of shrubbery. While not large, the pavilion can take on many aspects. The look of a pavilion depends on the shape of its top, its decoration and color as well as the layout of the surrounding garden.

The pavilion has a variety of forms. For example, there are pavilions that are square, hexagonal, triangular, pyramidal, octagonal, round, fan-shaped or semi-circled, and there are also pavilions that connect to one another. Moreover, pavilions can be found in a variety of locations—on hills, adjacent to water, on bridges or on the ground. The top of a pavilion, which typically draws a lot of attention, can take on many shapes. Usually the pavilion has a pyramidal top, but it can also have a gabled, saddle or parabolic roof.

The esthetic value of the pavilion, an important part of a garden, relies on two components. First, the pavilion must blend with the natural beauty of the garden. It is always located at the vantage spot that commands the best view. The pavilion may stand next to a building, quietly by a pond, above river stones and water, on a lawn,

opposite distant mountains, or near rockeries and ponds. The pavilion can be a very useful decoration, transforming a limited area into a vast expanse. When you are in it, you have an unobstructed view, as the pavilion usually doesn't have windows or a door. Instead, it is the dispersed pillars that bear the weight, so space inside and outside the pavilion is connected. In this way, the inside of the pavilion is integrated with the surrounding natural environment, and you feel that the garden is expanding.

This tetragonal pavilion sits on a rockey that has the appearance of a real mountain with a deep valley.

Here is the Heavenly Spring Pavilion in Humble Administrator's Garden, which highlights the artistry of gardens in southern China. This garden is one of the four most famous in China and is a world cultural heritage site.

The unique semi-circle pavilion is ingeniously built against a wall.

Octagonal Pavilion with Double-eaved Roof

This is a vantage point in Yu Garden, showing a place where the host and friends can entertain themselves, sit down for tea and write poems together. This pavilion complements Deyue (Moon View) Hall in the other corners of the garden.

Coupled pavilions look interesting and different.

In a large open space, the pavilion—like this tetragonal pavilion with heavy eaves—can also be larger giving the impression of stability and rustic simplicity.

6

Corridor

There are many ways to present the corridor in a Chinese garden. The corridor has several major functions. First, it directs the movement of visitors, and connects different parts of the garden. It also helps to integrate different elements of the garden, such as the pavilion and the wall and scattered scenic spots, into an organic whole. In addition, the extending corridor can separate scenic spots into near, medium-distant and distant ones, and make the garden look larger. Finally, the corridor provides both decoration and relaxation. It provides shelter from the weather, and visitors can rest in it, stand by the railing, and enjoy the view outside.

Corridors take several different shapes, and serve decorative and practical purposes. Looking at the cross-section, corridors can be open on both sides, open on one side, have a wall in the middle or have two stories. The roof may be flat or arched. The surrounding geography or environment also plays a role; there are corridors that are on a hill, enclosed by glass, on water, on a bridge, arc-shaped, cloister-shaped, winding or straight.

Whatever the shape, the corridor is unique in that it is winding and long, allowing for the combining of different scenic spots and creating a feeling of seclusion. With natural twists and turns, a piece of architecture can highlight the different layers of scenery and create enjoyment. The space of the corridor creates a special feeling, as its long, smooth and winding path follows the ground beneath it. Its openness allows for further interaction with nature. Strolling in the corridor, you feel you are indoors and outdoors at the same time, an engrossing and intriguing blending of sensations.

Winding Corridor

Corridor Open on Both Sides

Walking through the corridor at the eastern tip of the west part of Yu Garden, the view seems to improve as you venture further. Half of the corridor straddles the water, and the surrounding environment is serene, simple and elegant. The corridor is finely built and is covered by lush trees. Standing at the railings, you can see carp in the pond. Mountains, trees, water and a rockery come together beautifully.

Many long corridors in Chinese gardens are built by the river and, therefore, are usually called river corridors. Such corridors offer a view of the river and connect water and land. The corridor is usually situated adjacent to or over the river. It can break up the dullness and monotony of a partition wall, and enhance the artistic effect of the bank.

Xiaolian Manor is located to the west of the Eternal Bridge in Nanxun county in Huzhou. It is also called Liu Garden because it was the private garden of Liu Yong, the wealthiest person during the Ming dynasty. The garden occupies 17,399 square meters. The outer garden is centered on a lotus pond around which there are mountain rocks, pavilions, belvederes and railings. In the inner garden, there is a rockery made of lake stones and stately old trees. The long corridor, dotted with round pavilions, has an interesting and delicate structure, and the workmanship is top-notch. By the pond, you can enjoy the view of the lotus flowers.

Waterside Pavilion

In a Chinese garden, the waterside pavilion refers to a specific type of architectural feature, which sits on a platform that is half on water and half on land. Three sides of the platform are railed by low balustrades. The building in the center is usually rectangular, and the side facing water is open. Each side of the building has French windows that give an open and pleasant view. There are also chairs or long stalls. The building is either partially or fully on the water and supported by stone pillars or Tai Lake stones, so that water can lap against the bottom of the building. The water pavilion is not large and it looks agile and balanced. Its sides and shape are in harmony with the water's surface and the scenery on the bank.

The waterside pavilion should be built where it blends smoothly with the water and the bank, so that

The waterside pavilion should be designed in such a way that it protrudes over the bank into the river. In this way, it faces water on three or all four sides, giving those inside an intimate connection with the water, as well as a clear view of the surrounding scenery.

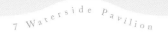

The waterside pavilion and the kiosk look similar, but the waterside pavilion is slightly larger. In its early years, the waterside pavilion was a wooden pavilion on a platform. It was a single-roomed structure with no internal partitions. Its doorways and windows were open, with no shutters, connecting the structure with the outside world. Like other types of structures, the waterside pavilion is an important esthetic element within a garden.

it naturally protrudes into the water. It should be close to the water's surface, and face water on three sides, thereby appearing dynamic. The Tai Lake stones used for the embankment should be placed at different heights and at appropriate intervals. The stones under the pavilion should not be arranged in an orderly or strict way. The supporting pillars should be as close to the bank as possible, so that the space under the pavilion gets larger and the pavilion looks taller.

The pavilion should be slightly above water so that it won't be flooded when the water rises. The pavilion, water surface and bank should be horizontally parallel, and the pavilion should be slightly above the water. The waterside pavilion should also be accompanied by white walls, windows with patterns, trees, fresh bamboos or red maples. In this way, the vertical and horizontal views are both satisfactory.

The waterside pavilion stands elegantly by the pond, facing the water and the bank. It is an ideal location for sipping tea, reading, painting and playing musical instruments. It is especially delightful to see swimming fish moving along with the reflected image of flowers on the pond.

The waterside pavilion can be built in a private, natural or imperial garden. In an imperial palace, the waterside pavilion retains the basic features of an ordinary one, while assuming characteristics fitting an imperial building. It is more sturdy and large, with more splendid and grand colors.

In a private garden, the pond is smaller, so the waterside pavilion is also smaller. Its side and shape should fit the area of the water. Half of it stands on water. There are railings around the pavilion and its furnishings are simple, delicate and elegant.

Kiosk

The kiosk, a perfect summer shelter, is built close to bluish water, with its shadow moving across the surface. In the Withdrawal for Contemplation Garden in Tongli town in Wujiang, Suzhou, the Coolness in Summer Pavilion stands close to the water. It is quiet and elegant. In midsummer, you can stand by the railing, enjoying the view of the red and green plants, as well as the refreshing fragrance. The pavilion is the ideal place for escaping from the summer heat.

The kiosk is common in gardens, and refers to structures located in open, expansive and quiet places. It is important to the layout and scenery of a garden. In terms of its look, setup and location, it is more flexible compared with the pavilion and corridor. It may have various styles, but is usually small, and built in the corner of a garden or beside a hall. The kiosk should be designed and sited in such a way that it is in harmony with the surrounding environment.

Many kiosk structures are presented in the form of a yard. The kiosk is in the center, surrounded by a veranda and walls decorated with patterns. In a yard of modest size, the kiosk creates a secluded and tranquil atmosphere. The look and form of the kiosk are like those of the waterside pavilion, although it does not stand directly on water. The Liangyi (Two-function) Kiosk in Yu Garden in Shanghai is an open kiosk that faces the water. The side facing the water is completely open, so that you can rest by the pillars or railings and enjoy the view outside. The kiosk, pavilion and corridor can be built together so that they form a variegated garden with structures of different heights.

In this picture, a lush green covers the pavilion, where one can stop to enjoy a refreshing view. There are flowers, trees and rockeries scattered by the water. Stepping outside the kiosk and walking up the steps of the rockery, you can look down on the garden and see a green pond of water. In summer, it is an unparalleled experience to come enjoy the coolness of the shade and watch the beautiful lotus flowers and delightful fish.

There are many pavilion-like buildings that resemble pavilions in small gardens but don't take up much space. It is most suitable to enjoy nearby scenery from inside, and the surrounding environment should be neat and elegant.

Here is the Nine-lion Kiosk, where the altitude is high and the surrounding view is uninhibited. It is a main area from which to enjoy the garden's scenery.

The Liangyi (Two-function) Kiosk in Yu Garden in Shanghai is an open pavilion that stands beside water. The side facing the water is completely open. There are only a few simple chairs between the columns where one can sit and rest. It is similar to the waterside pavilion in respect to look and function. The kiosk is usually built where it is serene and quiet. If it is built where the ground is higher, it provides a view of both nearby and distant scenery.

Chinese Belvedere

The belvedere sometimes stands at a prominent place in the garden where one can enjoy the surrounding view. On the rockery at the center of the west part of Humble Administrator's Garden in Suzhou, there is the Flowing on Green Belvedere. The belvedere is octagonal and its second floor has a pyramidal top. It looks like the belvedere is flowing on lush greenery, hence its name.

In Chinese gardens, the belvedere is mostly situated on the periphery, although sometimes it is in a prominent and central position in the garden, where one can enjoy the surrounding views. Located on a high slope, its tall figure forms the protruding part of the contour of the garden.

There are two kinds of belvederes in a garden: water belvederes and mountain belvederes. The water belvedere is further divided into two categories: adjacent to water or surrounded by water. The belvedere can be built by water that is vast and deep. This kind of belvedere should be tall and majestic, aspiring to touch the sky to command a view of the water and make the scenery all the more magnificent. The belvedere surrounded by water is in the center of the body of water, or on an island in the center. The belvedere occupies an important place on the island and becomes the main scenic spot.

There are four varieties of mountain belvederes: mountaintop belvederes, hillside belvederes, belvederes at the foot of a mountain

and belvederes by the cliff. The mountaintop belvedere is built on top of plateaus or high hills, which cover a large area and have an open and unobstructed view, so that one can see far into the distance. When you look at the belvedere from afar, it becomes a very beautiful and rich part of the mountain's contour.

The hillside belvedere is built into the hill wherever the shape is most suitable, and must meet the following requirements. First, there must be a good view. Second, depending on the slope, the hillside

This is the site of the Flower Deity Belvedere of the Ming dynasty. The current building, called the Wanhua (Ten Thousand Flowers) Belvedere, is finely decorated and furnished in the Qing dynasty. This impressive belvedere surely lingers in one's memory. On the first floor, there are four carved windows with patterns of plum blossoms, orchids, bamboo and chrysanthemums. In front of the windows, there are lake stones and a rockery. There is a winding corridor and railings encircling the belvedere. The environment is quiet and secluded. This belvedere showcases the style of gardens in southern China in the Ming and Qing dynasties.

The belvedere is located on a mountain or by water. The belvedere on a mountain is usually open on all four sides, looking grand and powerful, and presenting a clear and open view of the surrounding areas. In a belvedere by water, you can see the vastness of the water and the mirrored image of the sky on the water. It gives the impression that the water and the sky are conjoined.

should be crafted into steps of different heights, so that the belvedere becomes a destination point. Third, the look of the belvedere should be dignified and dainty, so that when one looks out, the surrounding mountains appear to be very small. It can be built on a hillside, open on three sides, with only one side of the structure reclining on the hill. Alternatively, it can be hidden in the hillside with only one side facing out, and the other three sides enclosed by sheer cliffs.

A belvedere can also be built where the hill meets the land. The belvedere at the foot of a mountain is usually built where the slope is not steep, in an open space and close to water, so that there can be gradations of view. This kind of belvedere is large, stable and solid. It blends with the mountains behind it, and together they form a beautiful outline. It also presents a grand and magnificent view.

A final choice for location is by the cliff, built on a precipitous and narrow ledge. The belvedere is connected by some horizontally placed building materials so that it is integrated into the cliff face. When you climb to the belvedere and see the sheer cliffs on both sides, it is as if you are next to an abyss, and the feeling is literally breathtaking.

The belvedere is a large and important building, which may have various shapes and looks. The size of the belvedere by the water should fit the size of the pond. Otherwise, a top-heavy feeling is produced. On vast water, a belvedere looks light and beautiful, producing a pleasing esthetic effect, such as the belvedere of Yu Garden in Shanghai, pictured here.

Guyi Garden in Nanxiang was carefully designed by Zhu Sansong, the famous bamboo carver from the Ming dynasty. It is large garden, with half of its original area taken up by buildings. There are fine and exquisite pavilions, belvederes and verandas. The Weiyin Belvedere is ten meters tall and consists of two sections. The lower section, called Dripping Water Belvedere, is classic and elegant, a good spot for enjoying the scenery outside.

10

Stone Boat

In classical Chinese gardens, there are structures called stone boats, which look like sailing vessels. Half on land and half on water, the boat's bow and both sides are connected to water by flat bridges. The bottom of the boat is made of stones. Where the boat is above water, it is supported by stone columns. The "cabin" is mostly wooden.

The stone boat is different from the pavilion or belvedere in that it has more pure esthetic value. It is unique because it looks like a boat but it is not. It has three sections: the bow, middle and stern. The bow is open and tall, so that you can see the scenery outside. The middle part is lower, an ideal place to relax or have dinner. You can also enjoy the view outside through long windows on both sides. The stern is the tallest; it is where you can gaze into the far distance. The stone boat has two stories. The upper story is like a tower, where you can simply enjoy the view, and the top of the cabin is light and exquisite. The lower part of the stone boat is a solid structure while the upper part gives one the sensation of rowing on a lake.

The stone boat is usually built where it can face water on three sides. In this way, you can have a broad view and feel a sense of delight in nature. However, there is one variety of the stone boat, called the boat hall, which doesn't have to be by the water. In fact,

When a pond is too small to row a boat on, a stone boat is a good substitute. Here, in Guilin Park in Shanghai, a stone boat lies across the limited water area. Its structure is fine and delicate. It also looks like a gaily-painted pleasure boat, which undulates over the green waves and stirs one's imagination.

its shape doesn't have to resemble that of a boat. You just need to build a door at the front of a long structure that has long windows on both sides, so as to imitate a real boat in an abstract way.

The Withdrawal for Contemplation Garden in Wujiang, Suzhou, was built during the Qing dynasty Emperor Guangxu's reign, which spanned 1885 to 1887. The owner, Ren Lansheng, returned to his hometown and had the garden built after losing his former position. The name of the garden signals this loss of status, reflecting on the past and correcting one's mistakes. Yuan Long, a famous painter in Tongli, carefully designed and built the garden. It has a fine layout, fits its environment, and creates grand scenery through minor objects. All the buildings, such as the stone boat here, are centered on the pond with their images reflected in the water.

The Lion Forest Garden in Suzhou is renowned for its rockery. The rockery has deep and secluded caves that are winding and resemble a labyrinth. There are also numerous peculiar stalagmites. The pond by the rockery is green and clear. There is a stone boat on the pond where all types of people will find beautiful scenery that appeals to them.

Humble Administrator's Garden in Suzhou, built during the Ming dynasty, is unique because of its water scenery. There is a stone boat called Xiangzhou facing the water. The upstairs looks like an ordinary building while the downstairs is like a kiosk. Across the river stands the Jade Kiosk, and the stone boat and kiosk set one another off. There is a large mirror in the stone boat that reflects the scenery across the river. This increases the depth of view, and provides a sense of delight as the scenery unfolds.

While immobile, stone boats can produce effects similar to being on a real boat. When standing by the railing and looking into the distance, you have a wonderful feeling that the sky is at the bottom of the clear stream and the boat is floating in clouds. On the other hand, when you walk away from the boat and look back, you may have the illusion that a small boat is trying to penetrate the shade of the willows.

11

Garden Path

In China, the garden path connects different scenic spots, and is designed to fit the natural environment. Well-designed paths can themselves become beautiful scenery. The path should be flexibly placed and reflect the enjoyment of nature, adjusting to suit the terrain and view. It can wind and become invisible sometimes. It should effortlessly guide visitors as they are appreciating the beauty of a garden.

Private gardens are small. Therefore garden paths sometimes need to be tortuous and winding. Sometimes you feel like you are at the end of the path, but suddenly you find the path continues. The charm of Chinese garden paths is that they wind and change naturally, and are full of rhythm.

In Chinese gardens, special attention is paid to the decoration of paths, so that they become a scenic spot in themselves. The decoration materials include black bricks, black tiles, pebbles, broken stones, tiles, and pieces of earthenware or porcelain. Shapes created by black bricks include the Chinese characters " 人 " or " 席 ," concentric circles, hexagons, concentric hexagons, elongated octagons, Chinese crabapple flowers and crosses. Shapes created by pebbles include the rectangle, square, rhombus, polygon and other miscellaneous patterns, including pomegranate, tropical citron with finger-shaped fruit, and bat. The most exciting of patterns is that made of colored pebbles carefully embedded in the path. You need to plan the design carefully first, and then use polished tiles and pebbles of different sizes and colors, including red, yellow, brown and black. The patterns are vivid and variegated, becoming one of the finest examples of the art of path design.

Garden Path Made of Pebbles and Broken Tiles

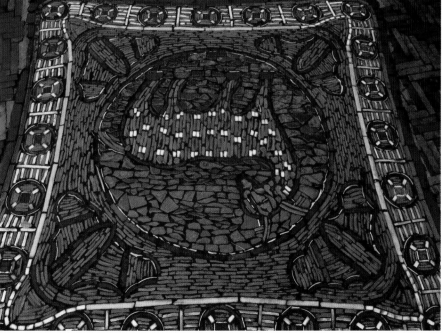

Paths in gardens often use common materials, such as gravel, pebbles, tiles or bricks, to create colorful and varied walkways. The paths may show patterns symbolizing auspiciousness or good fortune. Here are images of an auspicious pattern and a copper coin pattern. They are finely made and beautiful. Such furnishing approaches are often adopted in gardens in southern China.

Garden Path Made of Rectangular Broken Stones

Chinese attach special importance to having a safe trip on one's journey. This is shown in the design of garden paths. This pattern is made of pebbles laid in such a way so that you can see characters, written in seal script, representing good fortune and good luck. If you look carefully, you will find that each section has characters or pictures that show one's wishes or expectations.

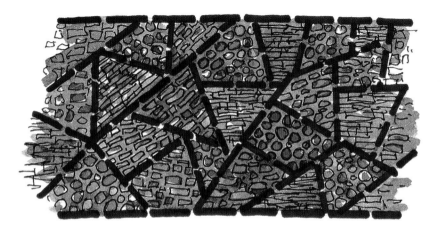

Path Made of Bluish Bricks, Broken Porcelain, Broken Yellow Stone Slates and Small Pebbles

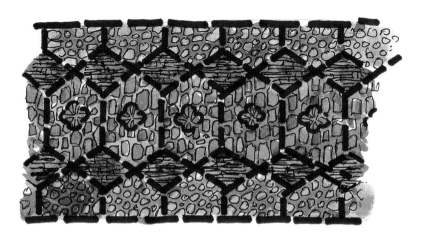

Path Made of Bluish Bricks, Pebbles, Broken Porcelain and Broken Yellow Stone Slates

Path Made of Small Bluish Bricks, Broken Yellow Stone Slates
and Small Yellow Square Stones

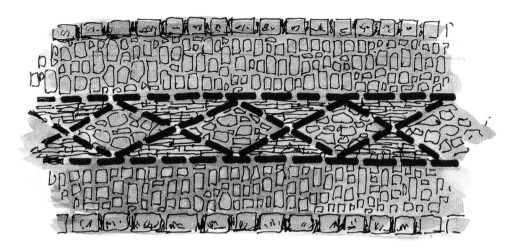

Path Made of Bluish Bricks, Broken Yellow Stone Slates and Small
Yellow Square Broken Stones

Steps

When building a garden, you can build steps on a steep slope or between places of different heights. Steps are part of the path, and connect different scenic spots. They make each part of the garden accessible, and they act like a tour guide, directing you to different areas. The art of the garden is all about naturalness. This also applies to the step. To make steps natural, they should fit the terrain and topography. They should be decorative and become scenic spots themselves.

Many materials can be used to build steps. For example, if you have a selection of Tai Lake stones from which to build rockeries, you can find among them some smooth stones that are a little convex. These make ideal steps, as water will not accumulate in the stones. Black bricks, broken stones or pebbles can also be used.

Step Made of Broken Yellow Stones and Pebbles

When building steps in Chinese gardens, you need to ram and pound them. There are at least two steps for each stairway—the upper is called the major step and the lower is called the minor step. There are no strict rules on the height of steps; they can be adjusted freely. What is important is that steps should be closely glued with mud, and the gradation of steps should be natural.

The stones used to build steps should be the same as the surrounding stones. The step should not look artificial or imposed upon the path. You may allow the steps to wind freely to take full advantage of surrounding rockeries and trees. Here is an image of steps in one corner of the Lion Forest Garden in Suzhou.

Step Made of Yellow Stones and Broken Yellow Stone Slates

Pebble Step with *Ruyi* Character and Pattern

Step Made of Stone Blocks

Chapter Four

Plants:
The Colors of Chinese Gardens

The appropriate selection and location of plants is a crucial part of creating a garden. A good design has several key components. The first is the selection of plants, including a combination of flowers and trees. Care must be used in order to ensure there are plants with different colors and growing seasons, creating a lively atmosphere for the garden. The second component is the appropriate collocation of plants with other objects in a garden, including buildings, rockeries, water, garden paths and walls, so that they work together to enrich the scenery. Plants play an important role in seperating spaces, decorating rockeries, ponds and buildings, organizing paths and setting off from the main feature. Third is the use of plants can as independent scenic spots.

Priority should be given to local plants, which are most likely to grown heartily and assume their full potential. Of course, plants from other areas can also be introduced in moderation to enrich the pool of plants. Plants should have a pleasing shape, large size, bright colors, long life and many distinct features. "Old" plants are of special value.

In private gardens, there is usually one of each kind of plant, to show the beauty of individuality. When grouping plants, those of different heights should be placed together in a naturalistic way, and in line with esthetic requirements. Besides being used within a structure or at the garden gate, plants of equal numbers can be placed symmetrically to keep a sense of balance. In wide and open spaces, rows of plants can be grown to separate space, and form a tree screen. Another often-used approach is putting more than three different plants together as a major or supporting scenic spot. In this way, their collective beauty and each plant's individual beauty are both highlighted. You can also grow several of the same plants together to exhibit their collective beauty and form a small bush, creating a different visual experience. For this effect, plum trees, bamboos, peach trees or flowering cherry trees are a good choice.

The following artistic guidelines are used in the collocation of plants:

Since the very beginning of the history of gardens in China, there has been special attention given to the arrangement of flowers and trees. It has become a serious and distinct discipline, not only related to botany, horticulture and other natural sciences, but also to art, painting, poetry and other humanities. The arrangement of potted plants, such as these at the Shanghai Botanical Garden, is just one aspect of this comprehensive field of study.

1. Plants naturally occur with different heights, colors and shapes, so you can highlight these differences to present a beautiful ecology. Plants have different postures. Some look neat and tidy, such as camellia and osmanthus. Some have a dynamic feature, such as plantain and pine. In collocation, we should not only stress harmony between plants, but also think of the relationship between dynamics and balance. We should pay attention to the vertical contour of plants, and ensure that plants have different heights, seem wavy and have a distinct rhythm. Arbors, shrubs, grass, flowers and cover plants should be combined. Trees in the background should be taller than those in the foreground, and density should be increased to form a green screen.

2. Plants with different florescence should be grown in different rows so that the beauty of a group of plants can last longer and seasonal changes in plants can be shown. The design should feature blooming flowers and wonderful scenery in every season—indeed, every month. For example, peach blossom and Chinese crabapple flowers bloom in spring, lotus and crape myrtle in summer, osmanthus and cotton rose in autumn, and plum and pine in winter. When people appreciate the beauty of plants, they care a lot about their colors and appearance. This does not only apply to flowers, but also the buds and leaves, which can show different shades of red, then they finally change from light green to blackish green. They bring enjoyment that endures longer than with fresh cut flowers.

3. Plants can play different functional roles in a garden. They can enrich the view and complement the surrounding structures. They can also partition the garden, mitigate the harsh outlines of buildings, and enrich the colors between buildings.

4. Plants also take on particular aspects depending on their location. On hills and rockeries, plants can show the change of seasons: the brightness of spring, the verdure of summer, the clarity of autumn and the gloom of winter. Over ponds, you can grow weeping willows that are slanting and full of change; for example, in hot summer, they are lithe and graceful. In water you can grow lotus, pond lily, duckweed and other water plants. At an inlet, you can grow some reeds to enrich the water area.

5. Creating a design for plants in relation to structures requires special attention. It is appropriate to grow plum blossoms in the front and back of the house, while at the back, you can also grow bamboo. Outside windows, you may grow plantains and slender bamboo. Against a wall, you can grow thorn bushes. Beside fences it's appropriate to grow chrysanthemum. Peony, Chinese herbaceous peony and rosebush can be grown in a flowerbed. At the gate and outside carved windows, you can grow trees that look handsome and grow slowly, such as sago cycad, bamboo, geranium and plantain.

To guide your selection of plants, some good choices for specific locations are listed here. Following this list, each plant is given a more detailed description, which also indicates other appropriate locations.

1. Beside windows: 1) crape myrtle, 2) camellia, 3) purple magnolia, 4) black bamboo, 5) red maple, 6) banana shrub, 7) osmanthus, 8) winter sweet, 9) plum blossom.

2. Wetland: 1) iris, 2) willow, 3) sasa fortunei, 4) lotus, 5) pond lily, 6) narcissus.

3. By the roadside: 1) hydrangea, 2) camphor tree, 3) paper bush, 4) Chinese flowering crabapple, 5) azalea, 6) boxwood, 7) pomegranate, 8) ginkgo, 9) red leaf cherry plum, 10) loquat.

4. On an arbor: 1) Chinese trumpet creeper, 2) Boston ivy, 3) rosebush, 4) wisteria, 5) ivy, 6) honeysuckle.

5. Beside stones: 1) China loropetal, 2) Bambusa multiplex, 3) sago cycad, 4) Japanese kerria flower, 5) firethorn, 6) five-leaved pine, 7) winter jasmine, 8) nandina, 9) podocarpus.

6. Beside a wall: 1) cotton rose, 2) hedge bambusa, 3) palm tree, 4) flowering cherry, 5) Arundinaria graminea, 6) magnolia, 7) gardenia, 8) Chinese rose.

Beside Windows

❶ Crape Myrtle

Crape myrtle, also called "a hundred days of red" in China, has clean and smooth trunks and twisting branches. It is a premium variety among garden plants. With its attractive figure, it looks very delicate and charming when it blossoms in summer. You can grow a pair of them at the gate of your garden, or grow one or many beside a lawn. You can also grow it near rockeries or among evergreens, so that it echoes the green color and forms a gorgeous scenic feature. It can also be planted in pots.

❷ Camellia

Camellia is an evergreen sub-arbor. When it blossoms, there are a lot of beautiful, dense flowers and lush, green leaves. It can be planted beside rockery or a pond, or it can occupy a prominent spot in a group of trees or a flowerbed. Because of the luxuriant leaves, many camellias can be grown together to form a fence or a screen to conceal unattractive spots. It can also be grown in flower pots and put in a study or on a balcony. During festivals, it is popular to place it in a parlor together with daphne odora as an auspicious sign.

❸ Purple Magnolia

Purple magnolia, a variation of magnolia, has a flower shaped like a Chinese painting brush. Its flowers and leaves blossom simultaneously. The back of its petals is purple while the front is light red. You can plant it in

❷

❸

④

the corner of a garden, beside a wall, on the roadside or on both sides of a door. It can also be grown in pots or jars. It can be planted together with magnolia and red camellia so that the purple, white and red colors interact with and set each other off. Purple magnolia brings the feeling of spring and is very charming and dainty. It is a fine variety within classical Chinese gardens.

④ Black Bamboo

Black bamboo, also called inky bamboo, has green leaves and purple trunks. It has a unique beauty. In a garden, it can be planted beside a wall, next to the gate, pavilion, kiosk, waterside pavilion or corridor, and planted together with rocks to decorate other scenic areas. You can also grow black bamboo beside a pond, by a lake or behind rocks. It can also be used as a screen to partition different areas of a garden. It is often grown together with pine and plum, and together they are considered the traditional "three friends of winter." It is also commonly planted together with plum, orchid and chrysanthemum. Black bamboo is very suitable to be planted in the ground, or in pots, which can be placed in a balcony or corridor. Potted black bamboo accompanied by rocks is very graceful and interesting.

⑤ Red Maple

Red maple has a dancing figure, with very fine leaves. In the autumn, the leaves turn red and become very charming. Its leaves are a major attraction in a classical Chinese garden in the autumn and winter. To form a colorful scenic spot, they can be collocated with other plants, such as ginkgo, China loropetal, red leaf cherry plum and maple. Several red maples can also be grown among pines and cypresses, to set off the handsomeness and beauty of the maple's colors.

Red maple can be accompanied by rockery stones, camellia, nandina or azalea. It can also be presented as the major scenic spot in a flowerbed, accompanied by sago cycad, China loropetal, azalea and camellia. Red maple may be put beside a pavilion, kiosk, waterside pavilion, gate, carved window, in the corner or on both sides of the garden gate.

❻ Banana Shrub

Banana shrub is a famous fragrant flower in China. This evergreen has lush leaves, and a neat and tidy look. It is often placed alone in a lawn, under a window or beside railings or bushes. Because of its fine fragrance, it should be put close to the door or window, and it can be planted singly or in large numbers. In this way, its beauty and fragrance can both be appreciated. It is a very popular garden plant in terms of fragrance.

❼ Osmanthus

Osmanthus, also called "nine miles of fragrance" in China, is one of the ten most famous flowers in China. It is a tidy and neat evergreen with a penetrating fragrance and sweetness. In a garden, it is often planted in pairs. The paired osmanthus should have a single trunk and a strong and beautiful tree crown, so as to present a pleasant image. It can also be planted beside a wall, window, corridor, rockery or rock-filled creek. A group of osmanthus may be planted on a hillside, plateau, lawn or open ground to form a strip. Osmanthus is often included in classical Chinese gardens for its beauty and fragrance.

❽ Winter Sweet

Winter Sweet is a unique flowering shrub in Chinese gardens—it blossoms when it is cold and windy. Winter sweet is round, and when it blossoms, flowers of a

yellow wax-like hue bloom on every branch, giving off a pleasant fragrance. It is often planted in front of a window, on both sides of the gate, at the corner of a wall, behind the house, by a lawn or near a rockery. A single winter sweet can be accompanied by bamboo, orchid and chrysanthemum to form a scenic spot. It can also be planted in a pot and placed in a study, or alternatively grown as a bonsai tree, providing high esthetic value. Winter sweet is a popular and valuable plant in terms of fragrance.

❾ Plum Blossom

Plum blossom is an important plant, especially in winter and spring. It is sturdy, quaint and elegant, and it never yields to the cold. Its color, fragrance and figure are all outstanding, and the flower is notable because of it long history and distinctiveness. In a garden, it is often accompanied by pine and bamboo, and they are known as the "three friends of winter." When it is planted with orchid, bamboo and chrysanthemum, they are traditionally termed "the four gentlemen." In most cases, a single plum blossom is grown in front of a window, beside railings, at the corner of a wall, near a rockery or a pavilion. A group of plum blossoms looks like a patch of fragrant snow. Plum blossom should be surrounded by trees with thick leaves. Otherwise, when its flowers wither, the view will be affected. In vacant places near rockeries, some plum blossoms may be planted to imitate a mountain forest. Plum blossom may be trimmed and put in a vase on a desk, bringing poetic splendor to the whole room. Plum blossom bonsais highlight the strength of its branches and its interesting figure.

❾

Wetland

❶ Iris

The iris is a wetland plant that is poetic and picturesque. Its slender, beautiful flowers resemble a kite or butterfly, and the elegant leaves are like swords. The iris is usually grown beside brook stones or a river. A group of irises can be planted near a rockery, at a bend in the garden path or on the rim of a grove. Irises accompanied by Tai Lake stones, yellowish brown stones and a pond present a pleasing esthetic effect. Irises can also be planted in a pot or jar, and placed in a bathroom or sitting room.

❷ Willow

In gardens with water, the willow is a must. The willow has myriads of branches, and a clean and handsome appearance. It has wonderful flowers and dancing catkins that bring special delight. The willow is usually planted beside a lake, pond, rockery or heaped stones.

❶

It is also often planted alternately with peach trees near a pond to form an image of red peaches and green willows. This combination is a popular feature of gardens in south China.

❸ Sasa Fortunei

Sasa fortunei is a short bamboo with dense leaves. On the green leaves, there are white and light yellow strips. At the end of spring and beginning of summer, when its leaves grow, it is especially eye-catching and brings a sense of wilderness. In a garden, it can be grown among rockery stones and by a pond or lake. It is often accompanied by geranium, camellia or azalea to form a scenic spot. It can also be grown as a bonsai and placed

on a desk or tea table. It looks neat and is very popular. It is a fine bamboo cover plant.

❹ Lotus

The lotus is a water flower with a long history of cultivation in China. It has large, brightly-colored flowers that look elegant and charming with a permeating fragrance. The lotus has green leaves that look gorgeous when blown by wind. The blooming lotus is charming and enchanting. The lotus can be grown in a pond, jar or bowl. It can be grown at the side of a pond or lake, or potted lotuses can be placed in a pond or lake. Potted lotuses are usually put in a sitting room, study or corridor so that their beauty can be appreciated. Lotuses in bowls can be placed on a tea table or shelf of curios. These delicate and exquisite lotus bowls are very popular.

❺ Pond Lily

The pond lily, also called the floating lily or sleeping beauty, has been very popular since ancient times. A fine and beautiful water plant, it is a perennial with thick, short stalks and a lot of leaves. It feels like leather and its shape is an ovoid or a heart. It has white, pink, red and yellow flowers, with white being the major color. It is especially attractive in summer. The pond lily grows better in a pond or on a lakeside. In a garden, it can be grown under a bridge or beside brook stones. It can also be potted and placed in a sitting room, kiosk or waterside pavilion.

❹

❻ Narcissus

The narcissus is a perennial plant with a corm. It may be unipetalous or polypetalous. The unipetalous variety, called the "golden cup and silver platform," has an extremely rich fragrance. The polypetalous variety, called the "exquisite jade," has unique flowers but a less notable fragrance. In a garden, it is the ideal flower to be placed by a pond or lake, or near a road. A group of narcissus can also be accompanied by mountain rocks, or placed beside a flower fence or in a corner. Its leaves have a soft and curving surface, which is graceful and appealing. When it blossoms, the fragrance is permeating and penetrating.

By the Roadside

❶

❶ Hydrangea

The hydrangea, a Chinese traditional plant, is both beautiful and valuable. The hydrangea is white as snow and has spherical flowers that bloom all over. It should be planted alone on an open lawn, or a group of hydrangeas can be grown by the road, on both sides of a building, or in a corner of the garden. Three or five of them can be grown near a rockery or a pond as a decoration. The hydrangea can also be accompanied by Tai Lake stones, China loropetal or azalea to enrich the garden landscape. A group of hydrangeas grown on a hillside or by a pond or pavilion creates a grand effect. Potted hydrangeas can be placed in a sitting room or study as a beautiful decoration.

❷ Camphor Tree

The camphor tree, an evergreen, has a strong, distinctive scent. Its leaves have a green hue, with grayish green backs. The tree crown is very large, and its shade blocks out sunlight. Due to its beauty and ability to provide shelter, it is often planted in Chinese gardens. A single tree can be planted in open space near a bower, kiosk or lawn, stretching out its branches to bring shade. It can also be planted near a sparse bush or can be accompanied by mountain rocks, rockeries or buildings. In autumn, some leaves turn red and become even more beautiful.

❸ Paper Bush

The paper bush, also called a golden girdle or knot flower, is a sheepberry of the daphne genus of the paper bush family. It blossoms in early spring with bright yellow blooms that gives off a faint and delicate aroma. It is often seen in gardens, and can be planted in front of a yard, on the roadside, on a corner or between a rockery and a pond. It can be grown singly or in large numbers. If it is presented as a background to set off evergreens, there is a lovely effect as its flowers bloom.

❷

❸

159

❹ Chinese Flowering Crabapple

The Chinese flowering crabapple belongs to the malus asiatica. Its tree crown is sparse, and it has thin and long stalks. The flower is a rouge color with pinkish white. It undulates in the wind, and when it blossoms, the flowers dangle and look beautiful and almost girlishly shy. It should be grown as a tuft or a group beside garden paths or a rockery, on a hillside, or at the rim of the lawn. It is often planted in a garden that blossoms in early spring.

❺ Azalea

The azalea is a famous flower that has a long history of cultivation and appreciation. In Chinese gardens, it is a basic plant grown in a flowerbed, under a rockery, in sparse groves or beside a pond. It is often planted together with geranium, fernleaf hedge bamboo, camellia or dwarf lily turf tuber. The azalea flower looks delicate and sweet. It has many varieties, such as spring azalea and summer azalea. It can also be styled in different forms as a bonsai, and is an ideal choice for placing on a desk or balcony.

❹

❺

❻ Boxwood

The boxwood, also called the melon seed boxwood, buxus sinica var vacciniifolia, and buxus harlandii hance, is often planted in Chinese gardens, with its leaves as a major attraction. It can be as tall as seven meters, and has dense branches and leaves. It is an evergreen, grows slowly, doesn't need to be trimmed often, and is very adaptable. It is often accompanied by mountain rocks or placed around the rim of a flowerbed. It can also be planted individually beside Tai Lake stones. It can be shaped in many ways, including in the shape of a ball, or trimmed and bound together to become a bonsai. It is beautiful both individually or accompanied by red maples.

❼ Pomegranate

The pomegranate is the first choice for a fruit tree in a garden, and has been popular for many hundreds of years. It appears sturdy and of rustic simplicity. There are splits in its tree trunks, which look mottled and interesting. It has brightly colored flowers. After the flowers wither, its fruit cracks, and the red pellets inside look like hundreds of agates. In a garden, it can be grown around the rim of a lawn or bamboo grove,

❼

❻

or it can form a scenic spot together with a rockery made of Tai Lake stones. Several pomegranates can also be planted in a flowerbed or in a corner. It blossoms in summer when many other flowers do not, so it is an important plant in summer. The pomegranate can also be appreciated as a bonsai.

❽ Gingko

Gingko has a majestic look, and is of both esthetic and practical value. Its uniquely shaped leaves are constantly changing color—verdantly green in spring, deep green in summer, and golden in autumn. Gingko has thick leaves and branches, and its large shade makes it an ideal shelter from sunshine. Gingko brings the feeling of autumn and its leaves are most beautiful then. It may be planted in a corner, beside a bower, corridor, kiosk or waterside pavilion. It can be planted individually, or a group of gingkoes can be grown together. It can also be grown together with red maple, taxodium ascendens, metasequoia and red leaf cherry plum, which have the same leaf characteristics, highlighting the grandeur of autumn.

❽

❾

❾ Red Leaf Cherry Plum

Red leaf cherry plum has leaves that are purple red throughout the year, and especially bright in spring and autumn. When it blossoms, it produces heaps of flowers. A group of red leaf cherry plums can be grown together to form a patch of red, expressing the feeling of autumn. It can be grown together with gingko, red maple and China loropetal to form beautiful autumn scenery. It can also grow individually in a corner, near a corridor or at the bend in the garden path. It can be set off by trees with light-colored leaves, to present a contrast between red and green, and highlight the beauty of its leaves.

❿ Loquat

Loquat doesn't wither, and is loved for its beauty and fruit. It has thick leaves, and in harvest times, it is loaded with a golden fruit. It is suitable to be grown in a corner in the garden, in front of a window or near the lawn. A group of loquats can be grown at the curb of a sloped path or near a lawn or a lake. It can also present beautiful scenery if accompanied by a rockery. In a garden, loquat beautifies the environment and also carries plentiful fruit.

On an Arbor

❶ Chinese Trumpet Creeper

Chinese trumpet creeper likes to attach itself to other things, climbing up to several meters. High up, it has a commanding view. Its flowers look like golden bells. They dangle in the wind and exhibit great charm. Chinese trumpet creeper has curvaceous branches with rustic simplicity. This climbing plant is often grown at a gate, covered with garlands, or near a shed, mountain rocks, carved railings, or wall, or at a corner in the yard. It can grow independently, becoming a large

tree over many years. It can be planted in a pot to bring greenness to a balcony, or it may hang under a cliff to bring extra delight. If it is crafted as a bonsai, it will appear aged yet vigorous and charming, which makes it quite a popular choice.

❷ Boston Ivy

Boston ivy is a multi-functional vertical plant often seen in gardens in southern China. Its large, thick leaves are red in spring and orange in autumn. It grows fast and requires little space, but can cover a large area. In a garden, it can grow on the ground, in a corner, on an arbor or on a fence. Or it may grow in a sparse grove on a hillside, above a trench or near a rockery or the garden gate. If the background wall is white and plain, several Boston ivies may be grown in front of it, the contrast of white with green bringing a feeling of decorative elegance.

❷

❸ Rosebush

When spring turns into summer, the rosebush goes into full blossom. It usually grows in a balcony or yard, or on a wall, fence or arbor. Its bouquets of flowers are enchanting. In a garden, a rosebush can be planted in the ground or in a pot. If it is grown in the ground, it may be accompanied by yellowish brown stones and Tai Lake stones, and placed in the crevices of a rockery, by a pond or lake, on a garden path, or in a corner. Rosebush is also used to enclose a garden or partition its space. It has thick branches and leaves when it blossoms, so it protects the privacy of the garden, and adds to its beauty.

③

❹ Wisteria

The Wisteria is a fine climbing plant often used to bring green to a garden. Wisteria has dense branches and leaves that can cover an arbor. When mature, its branches wind and coil, and its flowers dangle. It can be planted in many ways, for example, at the corner of a wall, on an arbor, wall or fence. Or it may be turned into a very tidily-trimmed bonsai tree. After years of trimming, it becomes an old tree, with curving and winding branches that give you a feeling of the ancient past.

④

❺ Ivy

Ivy is an ideal, vertically growing plant, which may be planted along a wall on the ground, or attached to a wall, mountain rocks or an arbor. It is also a cover plant that brings shade. It is quite adaptable and can endure a lack of sunlight. Ivy grows very well near wet stones and on the ground. It can also be turned into a bonsai and put on a bookshelf or desk, with its handsome branches and leaves dangling.

❻ Honeysuckle

Honeysuckle, also known as "winter-enduring vine" or as "gold and silver vine," often blossoms in spring and summer with a penetrating fragrance. In winter, its leaves turn a purple red. It is a half-evergreen twining vine. In a garden, it may be placed in a corner, in an area for vertically grown plants, on an arbor or fence, or as a cover plant attached to mountain rocks, a hillside or a pond. It can also be made into a bonsai, and is suitable as an indoor plant.

Beside Stones

❶ China Loropetal

China loropetal has dense branches and leaves. This popular plant is extremely pliable and has unique petals and darkish red leaves. When it blossoms, its color is like that of the red maple—gorgeous, enchanting and intoxicating. A group may be grown on a hillside or a lawn, or at the corner of a garden path. If it is planted along with red maple, red leaf cherry plum or other trees with similar tints, you will have a patch of trees with an autumnal flavor. Planting China loropetals among evergreens brings a bright red dot to a vastness of green, which is a special effect. It is also a good

material for bonsai, which can be put on a desk or in the sitting room.

❷ Bambusa Multiplex

Bambusa multiplex grows in a tuft. It is a dainty half-evergreen shrub with small, dense and featherlike leaves. It is suitable for planting beside a rockery or in a corner. Bambusa multiplex, Chinese rose and azalea planted together make a good scenic spot. It can be placed by a pond or lake. If it forms a set together with yellowish brown stones or stalagmite stones, they will become even more graceful and delightful. It is also elegant if accompanied by mountain rocks and placed near the gate, a wall or a kiosk. It may be grown as a bonsai, showing its beautiful leaves and elegant figure.

❸ Sago Cycad

Sago cycad is a valuable plant with a long history, and is appreciated for its beauty. This evergreen is also quite easy to grow. Its figure is dignified and simple. Its leaves, which look like the tail of a phoenix, are firm and evergreen. In a garden, it is often grown on both sides of a path or at the center of a flowerbed. A pair of sago cycads may be grown on both sides of a gate symmetrically. Three sago cycads of different heights may be planted on the flowerbed at a gate and accompanied with Tai Lake stones to form a major scenic spot. The scenic spot may also be accompanied

❷

❸

by seasonal yellow grass or flowers such as azalea or camellia to present a view that has three gradations— the tall, the middle and the low view.

❹ Japanese Kerria Flower

Japanese kerria flower has green branches and a long florescence. When it blossoms, it looks shiny and golden, with its green leaves and glittering yellow flowers glittering like a mirror. Its polypetalous flowers have a sweet smell. In a garden, a row of them may be planted beside a grove, rockery or a lawn. It can also be used to form a flower fence. When it is planted behind one or two Tai Lake stones, it becomes a beautiful scenic spot when in blossom. Its branches are good materials for flower arrangement.

❺ Firethorn

Firethorn has dense branches and leaves. In spring and summer, it has a lot of white flowers. In autumn, it has glaringly red round fruits that grow in strings, and dangle on branches for a long time. It is an ideal plant for appreciation. A tuft of firethorn can be grown near a lawn or at the bend of a garden path. A large number

of firethorn may be grown at the rim of a grove or on a hillside. The esthetic effect is excellent if accompanied by China loropetal, summer azalea or mountain rocks. You may also plant it individually, in front of a rockery or by a pond. It can be grown as a bonsai tree. Its spiraling roots, winding branches and full load of red fruits look delightful and appealing.

❻ Five-leaved Pine

Five-leaved pine is an indispensable plant in Chinese gardens. It looks dignified and robust, and carries the simplicity of the ancient past. The five-leaved pine can itself become ancient, and the older it gets the sturdier and more stoic it appears. In a garden, it can be paired with a cover plant or rockery. Usually a pine is grown

❺

❻

at the entrance of a gate to welcome and greet guests. The pine may also form a scenic spot together with plum blossom, red maple and azalea. A pair of pines may be grown on either side of a door. Five-leaved pine can be turned into bonsais of different looks and styles. Its bonsai may be placed in a sitting room, on a rockery or on a shelf of curios.

❼ Winter Jasmine

Winter jasmine is a rare plant that blossoms in early spring. It has long, slender, green branches and appealing golden flowers. In a garden, it can be grown by a pond, river, hillside, path or rockery. It may also form a flower fence to separate different areas. Winter jasmine, camellia, pine and cypress can be grown together to form a scenic spot. You can plant it near a waterfall, the dangling winter jasmine echoing the torrential water. It is also a good material for bonsai trees, which may be placed on a balcony or arbor to bring charm and attraction.

❼

❽ Nandina

Nandina is an evergreen shrub that never withers. It has sparse branches and leaves. In winter, it has a host of red leaves, and is loaded with shiny red fruit. In a garden, it is planted under a rockery or mountain rocks, in a corner, in front of or behind a house, or near stones in a pond. It can form a scenic spot with irises and azaleas. In festivals, people put it in a vase filled with water, together with winter sweet or pine as room decoration.

❾ Podocarpus

Podocarpus has a lovely dancing figure. It is verdant and fragrant and doesn't wither. In a garden, it can be grown as a cover plant, in a tuft or individually. It can also be planted on both sides of a gate or in a corner. It makes beautiful scenery together with red maple, camellia, azalea and stalagmite stones. It can be grown as a bonsai or tree bonsai, and placed in a sitting room or on a balcony.

❽

❾

6

Beside a Wall

❶ Cotton Rose

Cotton rose has large and bright flowers whose colors change three times a day. In early morning, the color is pinkish white. During the day, it is light red. At dusk, it turns deep red, and looks like a tipsy and shy girl with red cheeks, which is particularly charming. That is why it is also called tipsy cotton rose. You can plant it in a corner or near a rockery, a pond or brook, or accompany it with azaleas or camellias. It can also be turned into a flower fence or planted in a jar at home, on a balcony or in a corridor.

❷ Hedge Bambusa

The slender and beautiful hedge bambusa is a variety of bamboo that is often seen in the gardens of southern China. Its leaves are thick and droop, looking lovely while also helping to protect privacy. It is often grown near buildings, in a corner, or near a pavilion, corridor, kiosk, waterside pavilion, gate or patterned window. You can also accompany it with nandina, sago cycad

or azalea, and put in near several stalagmite stones of different heights and spacing. Hedge bambusa is often grown near a lake or pond, or used to partition the garden or surround the wall of the garden as a green fence.

❸ Palm Tree
The trunk of the palm tree is straight and upright. It has evergreen leaves that are as big as a fan. It is planted in many ways in a garden, such as in rows, in a tuft or in a group. Three to five palm trees of different

❷

❸

heights can be grown together in a well-spaced way. You can grow the tree in a tuft in the corner of a wall, beside a rockery, in a brook with rocks, in a pond, on the rim of a lawn, or in a corner of the garden. Two palm trees are often grown as a pair flanking a gate. When it is grown as a tuft or as a group, those in the back should be taller than those in the front so that the scenery has different gradations.

❹ Flowering Cherry

When the flowering cherry blooms, it is covered with hundreds of flowers, each vying with the others to be the most beautiful. It looks like a big green shade, which sways and looks splendid and gorgeous. In a garden, it can be grown as a cover plant, or three to five of them can be grown as a tuft to become a good scenic area. If the garden is not large, you can grow it individually in a corner of the wall or lawn. The flowering cherry does not thrive in a wet or humid environment, so it should be planted away from ground water. Before its leaves fall in the autumn, they turn red gradually. Accompanied with red maple or red leaf cherry plum, it reminds one of autumn.

❹

❺ Arundinaria Graminea

Arundinaria graminea is a fine garden plant with
drooping branches that are slender and dense. This
beautiful evergreen is suitable to grow on the rim of
a lawn, near a rockery or a corner of a wall, or at the
bend of a garden path. It can be placed near Tai Lake
stones or planted in a tuft or individually.

❺

6

6 Magnolia

The magnolia tree's dainty figure provides a charming decoration in the garden. Its flowers are as big as the lotus. They are white like jade, have the fragrance of orchids and look elegant, graceful and beautiful. In a garden, it can be grown in front of a building or at the corner of the lawn as a decoration. You can accompany it with peony, Chinese flowering crabapple and osmanthus to signify wealth and richness. You can grow it individually or in a tuft. If it is grown among evergreens, the colors of the flowers will be even more eye-catching, and present a good visual effect.

7 Gardenia

Gardenia is an evergreen, and in the blazing sun of the hot summer, its leaves are lush, green and fragrant. You can grow it in a corner of the garden, near a pond, on a hillside, or near a lawn or rockery. It can be grown as a cover plant or bonsai. A gardenia is a premium choice for domestic decoration. This fine, fragrant plant can be used to green, decorate and bring a sweet smell to a city.

⑧ Chinese Rose

The delicate and pretty Chinese rose is one of China's top ten flowers. Thanks to its long florescence, it beauty is often appreciated in the garden. There are Chinese roses of many different colors. In a garden, it is suitable to grow near a lawn, at the turn of a garden path or near a rockery. You can also grow it in a tuft to present a floral landscape, or as a bonsai in the sitting room or study.